The Saxon House of
ELDRED

Brass engraving of John Eldred etched in his alderman's gown, coif and ruff.

The Saxon House of
ELDRED

Nelson B. Eldred III
& J. Trevor Eldrid

Phillimore

1992

Published by
PHILLIMORE & CO. LTD.
Shopwyke Hall, Chichester, Sussex, England

© Nelson B. Eldred III & John Trevor Eldrid, 1992
Please direct all correspondence to
Nelson B. Eldred III
2885 Pine Grove Court
Marietta, GA 30067

ISBN 0 85033 822 0

Printed and bound in Great Britain by
BIDDLES LTD.
Guildford, Surrey

Contents

List of Illustrations

Acknowledgements

The authors wish to acknowledge gratefully the advice, help and contributions to the text, without which this book could not have been produced. In particular, Clare Gittings for her exemplary work on John Eldred of London and Great Saxham, and Luella Eldridge for her condensed version of this work; Ian Hulland (photographer) and his wife Marianne (journalist and researcher) from Bury St. Edmunds, Suffolk, for their splendid pictures and work on Great Saxham Hall, St. Andrew's Church, and Knettishall; John Denison Champlin for the article on the *Tragedy of Anne Hutchinson* (1904) and the republication of this work by William Henry Eldridge (1913). We are grateful indeed for the article on Pocahontas, the Indian Princess by Catherine Smiley Bartlett, who has provided an interesting account for the readers' enjoyment. We also thank those individuals and organisations who provided the illustrations for this book, especially Fabian Bachrach, 34; The British Library, 23; Brian J. Eldridge for the outstanding artwork on the Eldred coats of arms; Ipswich Borough Museums and Galleries, 18, 19, 22a and 22b; Jack Leonard, Braintree, Mass., 31, 32; The National Gallery of Art, Washington, 30; and The National Portrait Gallery, London, 21.

Introduction

The Eldred family is an old one, as its known history covers a period of more than 1,000 years. Its members are descended from the Saxons who came to Britain from southern Denmark in the fifth century. The name Eldred, with many modern variants such as Eldrid, Eldredge and Eldridge, survived the turbulence of the Norman Conquest, and the Middle Ages, and has deep roots in England and America today. There are more than 25,000 members of the Eldred-Eldredge-Eldridge family in America, and most of them can trace their lineage in an unbroken line for more than 550 years to John Eldred of Corby Glen, Lincolnshire, England.

The reader can expect to find a treasure of genealogical material on various members of the Eldred family. Included is the fascinating story of the Saxon-English background of the Eldred family and its coat of arms.

During the past hundred years, a host of dedicated people interested in the Eldred-Eldredge-Eldridge family have unearthed a mountain of priceless genealogical material. The main objective of this work is to share the fruit of their labour with everyone who is interested for whatever reason. Liberal use of their meticulous research notes and illuminating material has made this book possible. The material has been selected with great care – some of it is presented without change to preserve the original flavour.

Genealogy is a precise activity – not given to generalisations, trends or speculation in the final product. The principal characterisation of genealogy is documentation; the principal thrust of history, on the other hand, is that of overall perspective, of general movements, migrations, and philosophical and technical changes. However, documents written centuries ago have often been lost or are difficult for modern researchers to interpret accurately since language is not at all static. The pursuit of genealogical studies and the appreciation of significant findings leads one to understand that genealogy must be more than dates and names.

There is no doubt that future research will add to, perhaps subtract from, clarify, change and improve this genealogy. This is good. There are too many blank spaces, even after a century of work. The discovery of missing names, dates, places, and life stories remains a constant challenge to all interested researchers. Efforts are underway to identify members of the Eldred family who lived before the 15th century. The outlook for success in this endeavour is promising.

History

From the beginning of time, the period of ANCIENT history extends to the time of Charlemagne, who was crowned A.D. 800 (or, as some regard it, to the time of Alfred the Great, who was crowned A.D. 871).

From there the period of MEDIEVAL history, known as the Middle Ages, extends to the time of the start of the great Reformation, A.D. 1517 (or, as some say, to Columbus, 1492, or to Shakespeare's birth, 1564, or to the Spanish Armada, 1588).

From there the period of MODERN history extends to the present day.

John S. Wurts, *Magna Charta*, Part III, 609

Chapter One

Historical Background

Some historical background will help to illuminate the stage upon which our very early ancestors played their roles and on which they set the scene for us to play ours. As the great English playwright Shakespeare said, 'What's past is prologue'. An understanding of this background, including some geographical and political considerations, may be the only evidence showing who our ancestors were and how they lived in ancient and medieval times.

The last Ice Age began 10,000-25,000 years ago. After it receded, Britain was left an island. Soon thereafter, a Neolithic (New Stone Age) group called the Iberians found their way by rafts and canoes to 'Albion', the ancient name for Britain which was derived from the white chalk cliffs of Dover. They may have found people there who were known as Picts, whose origin remains shrouded in mystery. Basques now living in the Pyrenees are possibly the surviving remnant of the Iberians who once populated most of western Europe. The western migration of the Iberians to Britain was stimulated by the Celts who were entering their territory from eastern Europe. The Celts, along with the Indians, Persians, Greeks, Slavs and Teutons, were Indo-Europeans and had reached a higher level of social development than the Iberians. Their metal and bronze weapons were so superior to the stone implements of the Iberians that the Celts had no difficulty in destroying or absorbing the Iberians and pushing them further westward. Some of the Celts followed them to Albion and settled in the most desirable locations, forcing the earlier inhabitants to be content with the rocky hills of the north, the rugged areas of the west coast, or the island to the west now known as Ireland.

The Celts came in two great waves. The first were the Gaelic or Goidelic Celts – ancestors of the Irish and Scottish peoples. Salisbury Plain in Wiltshire was probably the early centre of population. Here the famous Stonehenge megaliths stand, and ancient footpaths worn into the chalk and limestone ridges which the Druids once trod radiate in all directions. Subsequently another tribe of Celts appeared, following the paths of the earlier group. These were the Brythonic or British Celts whose modern descendants are the Welsh.

The Celts were tall, fair-skinned and fair-haired, fierce and quarrelsome, and continually at war with their neighbours. They lived in houses made of wood or stone and used iron weapons and tools. They minted gold coins, traded extensively with the continent and mined tin in Cornwall. These latter Celts first appeared in Britain during the last millennium before Christ; the last of them, a Brythonic tribe called the Belgae, had begun to cross the Channel at least a generation before the time of Caesar (102-44 B.C.). The Celts worshipped many gods and their ministers were the Druids. They taught the doctrine of transmigration of souls, gave moral instruction to the young and practised human sacrifice. The influence they exerted over the

1

population was so great that when the Roman army invaded in A.D. 43 they found it necessary to completely obliterate the Druids.

It was in A.D. 43 that the Romans claimed Britain as the northernmost part of their Empire. To maintain the stability, security, improved communications, and more civilised life which Roman occupation brought to Britain, their legions had to be constantly on the alert. The wild and fierce Picts who lived in the highlands of Caledonia (now Scotland) refused to submit to Roman rule from the beginning. When attacked, they retreated into the rugged mountains where they waged such effective guerrilla warfare that the Romans were obliged to withdraw to the lowlands. After nearly 75 years, the effort to subdue them was abandoned and Emperor Hadrian had a huge wall built across the island, running from the mouth of the Tyne as far as the Solway Firth, to contain the Caledonians in their mountain areas. This wall marked the northern boundary of Roman Britain.

At the same time another barbaric tribe, the Scots, came from Ibernia (Ireland) in small boats, plundering, slaying, taking slaves and then quietly disappearing before armed assistance could arrive. These savage Scots eventually settled along the west coast of Caledonia giving it the name it bears today: Scotland. The Romans were also under continual pressure from marauding tribes in the north and west, and were constantly threatened along their eastern and south-eastern shores by the equally fierce and war-like Saxon pirates who were better equipped and armed than the Picts and Scots. At first they confined their activities to sporadic attacks, swooping down on some undefended coastal town and carrying off the slaves and property of wealthy Romans. Their custom of torturing to death one out of every 10 captives as a sacrifice to their gods ensured that they were particularly feared. These pirates came from the Jutland Peninsula and the northern coastal areas of Germany. They included the tribes of the Jutes who came from the upper part of Jutland, the Angles who inhabited Schleswig and Holstein, and the Saxons who lived around the mouth of the Elbe and further to the west. Their raids became more and more frequent and involved larger numbers of ships and men until, finally, the Romans were forced to build fortifications along the south-eastern and eastern shores at every point that offered a landing spot for the pirates.

Near the end of the fourth century, the Duke of Britain, Maximus, was proclaimed Emperor by his troops. To exploit his new position and authority he took most of his army across the channel in an attempt to conquer Gaul and Spain. Instead they were themselves apparently conquered, for they never returned and their loss greatly weakened Britain's ability to defend herself. Early in the fifth century the military leader, Constantine, was likewise proclaimed Emperor by his men and he, also looking for wider worlds to conquer, took his men across the Channel. Constantine was subsequently murdered and, like Maximus' troops, his men never returned. As the attacks and advances of the barbarians increased on all fronts, the Britons implored the Roman Emperor Honorius to send help. However, at this time (A.D. 410) Honorius was using all his troops in a desperate attempt to protect Rome from the attacks of barbarians who had broken through the fortifications along the northern boundaries of the Empire. Therefore, Britain had to provide its own defence and ceased to be a part of the Roman Empire.

After the departure of the Romans, the Britons were left to defend themselves against 'the men of the long knives', as the Saxons were dubbed, with their boar-crested helmets, woollen cloaks and long, ash-shafted spears. They regarded the invasion as divine vengeance for their sinful lives, but the root cause is thought to have been an ethnic upheaval in central Asia. In vain, the Britons appealed to the Romans for aid. 'The Barbarians', they cried, 'drive us into the sea, and the sea flings us back on the swords of the Barbarians.' But no help was forthcoming. Consequently, like the islanders themselves, the once populous cities, handsome villas and fine, straight roads, were all abandoned. It was not long before there remained scarcely a trace of Roman civilisation in Britain.

The Britons were not completely helpless after the departure of the Romans, for they had inherited a system of government and the rudiments of a military organisation which enabled them to prevent the Scots and Picts from making any permanent conquests of their territory. Increasingly heavy attacks by the Saxon pirates took their toll, however, and it became more and more difficult for the Britons to maintain order on the northern and western borders and at the same time keep the east coast under control.

Around the year 450 the British ruler, Vortigern, when beset by these problems, made a deal with a group of barbarians who had landed on the Isle of Thanet. These people were the Jutes, and they agreed to help Vortigern subdue the Picts and Scots in return for the island of Thanet as a dwelling place. Their joint military ventures were successful. The Jute population increased rapidly and soon they were demanding more space. Apparently Vortigern agreed to allow them some additional space in eastern Kent, but not satisfied with this they gradually occupied the entire coastal area of Kent. This was but the start of the gradual disappearance of the Britons from south-central Britain. The south Saxons settled in what came to be known as Sussex; likewise the east Saxons gave their name to Essex and the west Saxons to Wessex. In addition, the Angles took control over of the central and northern portion of the east coast. One group referred to as the North folk and another known as the South folk gave rise to the names Norfolk and Suffolk. These peoples later combined and became known as the East Anglians – and eventually lent their name to England.

The Britons did not surrender easily to the large influx of barbarians from Jutland and north Germany. In fact, in the early 500s, under Ambrosius, they beat the invaders so successfully at Mount Badon that the Saxons lost their ambition for further incursions – at least for a time. The successor of Ambrosius was apparently the legendary King Arthur. He was able to keep the various factions and tribes united and waged a very successful campaign against the invaders. For more than 30 years the Saxons were confined to their territories and a period of peace prevailed.

After Arthur's death, however, petty jealousies, vice and the lack of a strong leader divided the Britons again and the Saxons once more began a campaign of expansion. During this period the Britons all but disappeared from central Britain, as they were driven relentlessly west into the distant mountains of Wales and the infertile fields of Cornwall. Some even settled in Brittany but most were slain by the Saxons.

The Saxon invasion was the beginning of six centuries of almost continuous conflict for England. The Anglo-Saxons had to fight first for the mastery of Britain, then for supremacy among themselves, and finally for survival against the murderous Vikings or Danes. By the late sixth century, the invaders had conquered at least two-thirds of what we know as England, and their supremacy was soon admitted in the rest of the land. Very roughly, there was a preponderance of Angles in the north and midlands, of Saxons in the south and west, and of Jutes in Kent and Hampshire. Anglo-Saxons were firmly settled in the country by the year 600 although the term 'Anglo-Saxon' was not used until the ninth century to distinguish the Saxons in England from their kinsmen in Germany.

England was politically fragmented under the Saxons. A host of tiny kingdoms, or tribal areas, were governed by petty kings, in some instances no more than chieftains, or ealdormen as they were called. Gradually, however, these small states coalesced into a number of larger kingdoms – Northumbria, Mercia, East Anglia, Wessex, Kent, Essex and Sussex – known as the Heptarchy (seven kingdoms). Their leaders vied with one another for the coveted title of 'bretwalda' or 'leader of the British'. Kent was the first in the field, then came Northumbria, of which the greatest king was Edwin, whose name is commemorated in that of Scotland's capital city – Edinburgh. He was overlord of the English kingdoms that lay between the Forth and the Thames. Northumbria's supremacy lasted more than 100 years before it yielded to the kingdom of Mercia. Mercia was in the centre of England. Offa, its greatest king, made a clean sweep of the Romano-British who occupied Wales, and then built a vast dyke, still visible in places, to mark the border between England and Wales.

Early in the ninth century, Wessex, the land of the West Saxons and a late starter in the 'bretwalda stakes', achieved supremacy. For the first time a single kingdom stretched from the Firth of Forth to the Straits of Dover. Egbert, King of Wessex and Overlord of Northumbria and Mercia, assumed the title of 'King of the English'. Wessex, with its capital at Winchester, prospered and grew in influence, and the civilising effects of Egbert's wise leadership spread throughout the land. He was the first of a remarkably strong line of 'kings' which lasted for 264 years, apart from a period of 25 years of Danish rule from 1017 to 1042.

Storm clouds were gathering, however. Before the end of the eighth century the Vikings, from the land which is now Norway, had begun their bloody work. 'Never before has such a terror appeared in Britain', wrote a Saxon monk in 793 after the raid which destroyed the monastery of Lindisfarne off the Northumbrian coast. This was the first of many devastating raids which brought death and destruction to an England beginning to settle down to the prospect of a more peaceful life. Homes, villages, crops, churches and abbeys were reduced to smoking ruins. 'From the fury of the Norsemen, Good Lord deliver us!' was the woeful cry of the Anglo-Saxon peasants.

By 875 Wessex was the only surviving Saxon kingdom. It had been led to victory against the Danes by one of England's greatest kings – Alfred the Great. Soldier, scholar, man of genius and folk hero, he succeeded in containing the Vikings within the eastern part of England known as Danelaw. He was a vital link between the old England and the new, and out of the turmoil of the Danish wars a new national identity emerged. Alfred and his heirs, of whom King Eldred was one, raised the status of England's island people to a level previously unknown to the greatest powers of Christian Europe.

* * * * *

Edward I, known in history as Edward the Confessor, was king from 1042 until 1066. As a child, he had lived for a time at the court of the Duchy of Normandy. The Normans were a mixture of Scandinavian and French people who lived in a region of north-western France bordering the Channel. While there, Edward became a good friend of his cousin, William, who later became Duke of Normandy. Throughout his life, Edward showed more loyalty to the Normans than to the English. Edward had also spent part of his childhood in Ely monastery and, consequently, retained a strong predilection for piety.

When Edward died in 1066, the English nobles asked Harold, head of the most powerful noble family in the land, to be their king. Before his death, however, Edward had secretly promised the throne to his cousin William, Duke of Normandy. William, upon hearing of Edward's death, began making preparations to claim the throne that the English nobles had given to Harold. In October 1066, the armies of the two men, neither of whom had a wholly legitimate claim to the crown, met at Hastings to determine in battle who should be king. William won and became known as William the Conqueror. Harold was slain by an arrow. An important result of this Norman Conquest was the influx of French-Norman culture into England; for example, many French-Norman words soon became part of the English language.

William was crowned William I, King of England, on Christmas Day 1066 in Westminster Abbey. He refused to be consecrated by Stigand, Archbishop of Canterbury, but instead gave this honour to Ealdred or Aldred, Archbishop of York. Ealdred administered the coronation oath, anointed William, and crowned him before many of the English and Norman nobility. During the ceremony, Normans stationed outside the Abbey thought the shouts of acclaim were shouts of violence. Their reaction was to attack the crowds and set fire to nearby houses. The English rushed out to save their homes and William began his 21-year reign amid the din of crackling flames and the screams of angry, fire-fighting Englishmen. Archbishop Ealdred died a few years after William was crowned and left his malediction to the monarch because of his harsh, tyrannical rule over his English subjects.

Initially, William retained existing governmental organisation and local customs throughout England. Although his administration was relatively benign, many English people resented the foreigners. In 1068, while William was on a visit to Normandy, some English earls staged local uprisings. William returned to restore order in his kingdom and, although he treated the rebels leniently, the northern earls rebelled again the following year. Enraged, William carried out savage reprisals upon the people living between York and Durham, an area about the size of Connecticut. William's forces devasted the area: not a building was left intact nor a resident alive. As much as 17 years later, Domesday Book records that scores of villages were still completely deserted.

Being now indisputedly in control, William distributed the best land to his Norman aides and encouraged them to build castles and fortresses for defence against the hostile population. No two of the more powerful nobles were allowed to own land adjacent to each other, and William kept large tracts as hunting preserves for himself. His government dominated the conquered without mercy, and the Saxons suffered in every way.

To establish a definite and orderly basis for assessing and collecting taxes, William in 1085:

> ... sent all over England into ilk Shire his men, and let them find out how many hundred hides were in the Shire, or what the King himself had of land or cattle in the land or whilk rights he aught to have ... Eke he let write how mikle of land his Archbishops had, and his Bishops, and his Abbots, and his Earls, and what or how mikle ilk man had that landholder was in England in land and in cattle and how mikle fee it was worth ... so there was not a single hide nor a yard of land, nor so much as – it is a shame to tell, though he thought it no shame to do – an ox nor a cow nor swine was left that was not set in his writ.

This quote is taken from the *Chronicles of a Monk of Peterborough*. The results of the listing were embodied in what became known as Domesday Book – so called because one could no more hope to obtain relief from the taxes specified in it than from the last judgement. Domesday Book was completed in 1086, a year before William's death in Normandy in a riding accident. It was, unfortunately, used as the basis for taxation long after the information it contained was obsolete. Two volumes of the original Domesday Book can be seen today in the Museum of the Public Record Office in Chancery Lane, in London.

Robert, the eldest son, received Normandy as a separate kingdom; William Rufus, the second son, was crowned King of England in 1087 by Archbishop Lefranc; and the youngest son, Henry, was left with only an inheritance of money. William Rufus, was killed while hunting – his tyrannical rule had lasted 13 years. He was succeeded by his younger brother, Henry.

William I (the Conqueror) had divided the country into shires as the largest political subdivision and introduced Norman feudal personnel (knights), monies and other considerations in return for his right to hold land. Although landholders had full use of the land, they didn't actually own it. The king retained *de facto* ownership and thus was landlord of the entire kingdom. Landholders agreed to provide him with a specific number of mounted, trained and equipped knights for 40 days each year; this was known as the 'knights fee'. To acquire this fee the landholders sublet some of their land to mesne tenants who, in turn, allocated a portion of their land to smaller tenant holders. A vassal held land from his lord and his lord's lord was called the overlord. The land so held was known as a fief. A man might be vassal to several lords, but one would be his liege lord to whom he swore primary allegiance. Most of the tenants (serfs) were not greatly affected by these changes as they were already bound to the land involved.

Most Englishmen lived on farms (manors) in the 11th century; the few cities were small. The system of village government, customs and inter-social relationships varied widely in various parts of England, but its basic structure in Lincolnshire, Norfolk, Suffolk and Essex, the home of known Eldreds who emerged in the early 15th century, was about the same. Farm land was under the jurisdiction of a lord whose manor consisted of an area roughly the size of a New England town. 'Manor' initially referred to the entire land holding; later it meant only the actual dwelling place.

A villager's status in an East Anglian village generally depended on two conditions: the amount of land he held and whether he was a freeman or villein. The villein was a bondsman; that is, he was 'bound' to the land, and if he left it he would be declared an outlaw. Often a freeman might have few or no land holdings while a villein might have extensive ones. However, a freeman, though he might be poor in land, was usually accorded respect and privilege that was not due a villein.

The villein was not only bound to his land, but he could not marry without land. Under the existing system of primogeniture, only the oldest son could inherit. For the others, the only method of obtaining land was to marry a land-owning widow, inheriting as next in line if the eldest son died, clearing waste or new land (this only with the lord's permission), or occasionally obtaining from the lord land that had become vacant and had reverted back to his control. Land could also be obtained through military duty. Those who did not have any land could go into a trade as, for example, a smith or miller.

The system of primogeniture, and the requirement that a man must have land in order to marry, acted as a brake on population growth. Although new areas were being cleared, there was a shortage of productive land and the population increased very little in the 13th century. The wool industry did expand, however, as there was a great demand on the continent for fine English wool. Weaving was a cottage industry and provided the villeins with a cash income. Their rapidly increasing flocks of sheep could be grazed on fallow fields after cattle had been pastured on them, and also on waste land. The more successful wool producers were soon able to employ assistants called 'undersettles' who lived in small cottages on the villein's messuage.

The villagers, to some extent, practised soil conservation. They usually divided their croplands into three fields, one of which was allowed to remain fallow each year, one planted with spring crops and the other with winter crops. These plantings were rotated, and the fallow field provided pasturage for the stock. The width of the fields varied, depending on the number of villagers and the amount of land. The length, however, was usually consistent as it was determined by the distance a yoke of oxen could plough before they needed to rest. It was desirable to minimize the number of times the ploughman had to turn the oxen and plough around. This long furrow eventually became standardised at 660 ft. and was called a furlong. A strip of land a furlong in length and a rod in width was called a rood. A yoke of oxen could normally plough four roods in one day and this became known as an acre. Hide, the term for a larger area of land, was derived from the Saxon word for family and meant the amount of land necessary to support one family. This was about 120 acres but varied in different parts of the country, and sometimes even in the same 'hundred', depending on the character of the land.

In the 14th century, population pressure for more land, ability of the villein to accumulate cash and, most importantly the Black Death, combined to initiate the downfall of the feudal system. Almost half of England's population fell victim to the plague in 1348-9. This created a severe labour shortage, and consequently the villeins were in a position to demand more generous terms for their services from their lords. Some of them became molmen – men who paid rents in lieu of work services. The more astute enlarged their holdings and increased the number of their employees.

Inflation resulted from this emerging money economy – labour, goods and services all cost much more. This caused many to seek new livelihoods and gave rise to new classifications in the social order. The most numerous was the 'yeoman' class which included three prosperous sub-classes: the freeholder who farmed his own land, the capitalistic 'gentleman farmer' who might own several farms operated by his employees, and the peasant farmer who had his land on terms not subject to change. The typical yeoman was a frugal, hard working farmer and a shrewd businessman. Some increased their profits by buying grain when prices were low and holding it until prices rose. This practice was discouraged by law and it sometimes resulted in the yeoman having to pay a fine. In East Anglia most of the yeomen spent at least part of their time in the cloth industry. Many of the New England immigrants came from this area.

Another class that became prominent in this era was that of the 'squire'. When Henry VIII broke away from the Catholic Church, church holdings were made available for purchase. The squires often took the place of nobles who had been forced off their land by economic conditions. 'Squire' was not a legally recognised title; it was merely a recognition of the status that certain yeomen had achieved.

A 'gentleman' was one who had been granted the right of gentility by the Heralds' College, which depended on the possession of a substantial amount of property. Eventually some of the more successful 'gentlemen' formed organisations similar to modern corporations. One of the these, called the Merchant Adventurers, engaged in trade from England to the Levant and India and was the forerunner of the East India Company.

From the time of William the Conqueror to the beginning of the 15th century – a period of more than 300 years – there was little change in the basic social order in England. The 15th century ushered in the establishment of commercialism and slight traces of industrialisation, opening up opportunities for the improvement of living conditions. It was in this expansive period of opportunity that the Eldred-Eldredge-Eldrige family, with its ancient Saxon roots, began to flourish again.

Chapter Two

Saxon Heritage

Wherever the descendants of the Saxon race have gone, have sailed, or otherwise made their way, even to the remotest regions of the world, they have been patient, persevering, never to be broken in spirit, never to be turned aside in enterprises on which they have resolved. In Europe, Asia, Africa, America, the whole world over; in the desert, in the forest, on the sea; scorched by a burning sun, or frozen by ice that never melts – the Saxon blood remains unchanged.

Charles Dickens

Now let us go back to the beginning of the Saxon period and consider what manner of men were these ancestors of ours, how they lived, and how they managed their affairs.

Arthur Bryant, in his book *The Medieval Foundation*, tells us that they were great seamen and warriors: 'Coming from desolate coasts and wind-swept mud flats, gale and storm were in their blood'. Their boats were some 70 or 80 ft. long and 12 ft. wide. They were undecked, mastless, with a paddle at the stern for steering, and 14 or 16 oars a side. Our Saxon ancestors loved fighting. Bryant again: 'They loved the symbols of death and courage: the raven who follows the host with his beak dripping with blood, the hungry hawks hovering over the battlefield, the funeral pyre hung with shields and helmets'. This bloodthirsty appetite is well illustrated by a passage from the *Anglo-Saxon Chronicle* describing the Saxon invasion:

> Public, as well as private, structures were overturned; priests were everywhere slain before the altar; the prelates and the people, without any respect of persons, were destroyed with fire and sword. Nor was there anyone to bury those who had been thus cruelly slaughtered. Some, taken in the mountains, were butchered in heaps; others, spent with hunger, came forth and submitted themselves to the enemy for food, being destined to undergo perpetual slavery, if they were not killed on the spot.

Happily the Saxons did have another, less violent, side. If not, many of us would probably now be reluctant to claim them as forebears. They were great farmers – by far the best England had known. Bryant writes:

> Barbarians though they were, they were more patient, industrious and methodical than any of the peoples they had conquered. They had a genius for cooperation; they worked together just as they rowed and fought together. They shared the same ploughs, helped to cultivate one another's land and followed common rules of tillage and forestry.

They were as loyal to each other as they were ruthless to the enemy. Traitors, cowards and deserters were hanged from the nearest tree.

The Saxons had little use for towns; with the possible exception of London, capital of the East Saxons, they neglected those that had been vacated by the Romans. Instead, as Tacitus wrote of the Germans, 'they dwelt apart and at a distance from one another'. The Saxon peasants lived in clusters of humble, tent-shaped huts, with a hole in the thatched roof to let out the smoke. These closely-knit communities, known as tuns, whose names still mark the maps of England, were usually sited near streams, in clearings of the forests that covered most of England at the time.

These early Saxons in Britain seem to have retained many of the German customs and ways of life acquired before the invasion. They were, for instance, like their descendants have ever been, great upholders of the concept of personal freedom. A 'free-necked' man was one who had never bowed his head to a lord. The family was the most important unit of Saxon society, and the strongest social tie was the tie of blood. Communal witness to a man's character lay at the root of tribal law. If a man injured another, or stole his property, compensation was exacted not from the individual, but from the family. This compensation was known as 'blood wite'. The amount payable, the 'wergild', depended on the social rank of the man injured. A ceorl, the lowest degree of freeman who owned land, commanded a lower wergild than, say, his lord, probably a thane, who was a larger landowner or a minor nobleman. Some, indeed, with special duties to the king, ranked senior to a thane, with a commensurate wergild. An ealdorman, whose lands were extensive, was often a king in his own right. An odd feature of Saxon tribal law was the statutory rate for the crime. It was, it seems, cheaper to shed blood on week-days; at weekends the fines were doubled!

Village business was transacted at the village moot where the heads of families met under some local feature, such as a large tree, or on a hill. Tribal business, including justice, was dealt with at a senior assembly called the folk moot, presided over by the king. A king's election was based on a combination of custom and tradition. When all of the small kingdoms had merged into one unified state, it was only the leaders who conferred together, in a form of privy council. This meeting of wise men was known as 'witanagemote'. After such meetings, these men undoubtedly feasted together, much as conferees do today, and indulged in what Tacitus describes as 'a liquor prepared from barley or wheat, and brought by fermentation to a certain resemblance to wine'. The Anglo-Saxons coined a word for this still popular brew. They called it ale.

* * * * *

The early Saxon settlers were pagans subscribing to the faith of all the Nordic peoples. Their chief god was Odin (or Woden), the god of war, from whom the Saxon kings traced their descent. Thor was the god of thunder; Fria, goddess of joy and fruitfulness; Soetere, god of hate; and Teu, god of the dark. The names of these ancient gods survive today in the names of the days of the week: Tuesday (from Teu), Wednesday (Woden), Thursday (Thor), Friday (Fria), and Saturday (Soetere). Sunday and Monday, the sun's and the moon's day, are also of Saxon origin. The Christian festival of Easter is named after the Saxon goddess of spring, Eostre. The Saxon's heaven was Valhalla. Death in battle ensured automatic admission to that desirable retreat, where the fallen warrior divided his time between fighting and feasting.

The Saxons were superstitious and believed in elves and fairies, as some still do on the Isle of Man where there is a bridge over a stream which tradition associates with the Little People. To cross without paying respects to them is to court bad luck, and, surprisingly, many people still observe this old tradition. The name Alfred is derived from words meaning 'elves counsel'.

Christianity came to Saxon Britain in 597, when St Augustine landed in Kent, converted the king and founded the great cathedral at Canterbury. He was the first of several able and dedicated missionaries sent from Rome to bring Christianity to the Saxon kingdoms. The original Romano-British tribes had, of course, become Christians before the legions left Britain. The new wave of missionaries laid the foundation for the English Church, and for its culture, knowledge and civilised values. It was under the tutelege of the early Church that the warring tribal communities became a nation.

Paulinus, one of St Augustine's men, converted Northumbria in 625; Aidan, a monk from the Scottish island of Iona, established a Christian settlement on Lindisfarne and went on to convert the kingdom of Mercia. Wessex soon followed, and Britain again became a Christian land. These early churchmen were a band of remarkable men. One, in particular, deserves special mention for the powerful influence he exerted on the growth of the Church in England. He was a Greek, Theodore of Tarsus, Archbishop of Canterbury, who travelled throughout the land consolidating, diffusing learning and encouraging the development of sacred music. Another Christian monk, who is perhaps the best known figure from Saxon England, was the Venerable Bede of Jarrow (673-735). He wrote the first ecclesiastical history of England, one of our most important sources of information for this period. His epitaph in Durham Cathedral reads: 'He was an Englishman, born in an obscure part of the world, who by his knowledge enlightened the whole universe'.

In the 10th century there was another outstanding man of the Church who carried out a series of reforms that were urgently needed, as the clergy had grown lax about observing the rules of their calling. He is of special interest to us because he rose to prominence as the minister to King Eadred. His name was Archbishop Dunstan. A mystic, saint and musician, he initiated the earliest form of service that is still used at the coronation of Britain's kings and queens.

From the Church our Saxon forbears learned not only Christianity, but also the humanities and the arts, among them the important, but by then forgotten, art of writing and record keeping. Barbarian rulers were shown how to govern justly by men who had received such training in the Church. In return 'the king guarded the Church's property, made gifts of land and treasure to the monasteries and conferred high office on its clerics – Dunstan is an instance of this – for they were the only men in the realm who could read and write' (Bryant). The oldest work of literature in English is the epic poem *Beowulf.* Although the author is unknown, the likelihood is that he too was a monk or cleric. King Alfred taught himself to write and translated several Latin books into English. He is also credited with having begun the *Anglo-Saxon Chronicle.*

A measure of the rapid advance in learning made in Saxon England is illustrated by the story of Alcuin, a Northumbrian scholar, who was invited to the court of

Charlemagne to teach. So it was that Charles the Great, ruler of all western Europe, except Spain, turned to Anglo-Saxon England for instruction. Certainly, England was by now a storehouse of knowledge. The city of York, where Alcuin was educated, had the largest library north of the Alps – 'had', that is, until it was sacked by the Danes.

Despite the turmoil of being in an almost continuous state of war, our Saxon forbears developed creative and artistic skills, often of a high order, as shown in some of their surviving artefacts. The British Museum in London has assembled a varied and interesting collection of examples of Anglo-Saxon workmanship which merits study. Many of the items are from a remarkable treasure trove recovered in 1939 when a Saxon burial ship was found near the Suffolk coast at Sutton Hoo. This is near Ipswich, a place with many Saxon, and indeed Eldred, associations. The collection includes weapons, belts, buckles, brooches, jugs, urns, drinking horns, even purses. Made of silver, bronze, bone, glass and iron, the artefacts have survived for more than 1,000 years. Now cleaned and polished, many look as good as new.

During excavations at Coppergate in York in 1982, an important archaeological find, described as the most important in the city in this century, was turned over by a mechanical excavator. It is an Anglo-Saxon helmet, the best preserved of its kind ever found in England, and believed to have belonged to a Saxon nobleman in the days when York was an important centre of the kingdom of Northumbria. The helmet consists of iron plates riveted together to form the head piece, hinged sides to protect the cheeks and a noseguard. The forehead is protected down to the eyebrows, and the helmet is decorated with thin strips of copper alloy, giving the appearance of a shining mask.

Perhaps the most exquisite of all examples of Anglo-Saxon craftsmanship is to be found in a book known as the *Lindisfarne Gospels*. Lindisfarne is on Holy Island, off the coast of Northumberland, to which it is today connected by a causeway, and is one of the earliest centres of Christianity in Saxon England. Ruins of the monastery, sacked by the Danes during their first raid on England in 792, survive. It was here that this beautiful book was produced. The fine quality of the penmanship, as demonstrated in the illumination, is a most impressive example of the skill and dedication of Anglo-Saxon artists. Eldreds should make a point of inspecting this book in the British Museum, for it was a monk named Aldred who translated the Gospels into the native language. His word-by-word translation is written neatly above the Latin text.

Anglo-Saxon women are believed to have been expert weavers. William the Conqueror found that English clothes were far superior to those of the French. Not only was the cloth of better quality, but, to satisfy Saxon tastes, the clothes were colourful. King Alfred evidently approved of colour in dress for it is recorded that he gave his grandson 'a scarlet cloak, a belt studded with diamonds and a sword in a golden scabbard'. Ecclesiastical vestments were richly embroidered with gold and coloured thread. Bede tells us that the scarlet dye used by the Anglo-Saxons was made from cockles, of which there was, he writes, a great abundance. In this connection, an interesting object found in a Saxon grave points to the care of clothes: a work box made of gilt bronze and containing thread, wool, linen and needles.

* * * * *

The discovery of everyday items, such as jewellery, combs, spoons and workboxes, brings the Saxons within the compass of our imagination and understanding. They help us, who use many of the same objects today, to identify more easily with our kinsmen of long ago. Can we go a stage further – can we pick out people in the modern world recognisable as typically Anglo-Saxon? Only with great difficulty, if at all. The modern Englishman, like the modern American, is an amalgam of so many races – Celt, Saxon, Dane, Norman, Huguenot, Dutch, Spanish, to name a few – that it seems most unlikely that the true Saxon has survived. The historian G. F. Scott Elliot, who was writing at the beginning of this century, thought that the Saxon could still be found among the agricultural labourers of Essex and Sussex. Here, he said, you would find a man who combined a strong bodily frame with that grand solid obstinacy of character which was so invaluable in building the British Empire.

Mr. Scott Elliot was writing at a time when Britain was at the apogee of its imperial power. He goes on:

> The Anglo-Saxon is perhaps, if it is possible, more difficult to move when he is upon the battlefield than anywhere else. Over and over again he has gained the victory when, by all rules of warfare, he should have been utterly defeated. He cannot be called either bright or talkative, but he is by no means a fool, especially where his own interests are concerned. But that taste for beer which he first acquired in the forests of Germany still clings to him, and does not improve either his general intelligence or his prospects in life.

Were the same author writing about the Anglo-Saxon of the present day, one cannot help feeling that he might well revise some, if not all, of the comments he made three-quarters of a century ago!

Although it is unlikely that any of us have pure Saxon blood in our veins, we are, nevertheless, inheritors of a wonderfully rich legacy. In addition to the land itself, and the language, our Saxon legacy embraces a whole range of customs and attitudes, of places and buildings, all of which have come to be regarded as 'typically English'. It is a legacy that, over the years, we have come to cherish and, when need be, to fight for.

The very landscape of England was fashioned by Saxon farmers. The English village was created when the barbarian invaders of Roman Britain, weary of battle, turned to husbandry and began the awesome task of clearing England's primeval forests and moorlands. 'Field', 'ing', 'ham', 'hurst' and 'ton' (from 'tun') are still among the most familiar suffixes in English place names, and they serve as reliable indications of a Saxon origin, just as the suffix 'by' denotes a Danish one. Saxon lanes, too, have been winding through the beautiful English countryside for 1,500 years or more.

How, in fact, did the villages become established? Charles Bradley Ford suggests in an article that the first centres of Saxon conquest multiplied quickly. The son, or perhaps the servant, of a thane would receive permission to make his own clearing in the forest. Here he would build a log house, much in the style of an American back-woods settler in more recent times. Later, he would add supplementary buildings and finally surround the whole with a stockade which raised the settlement to the status of a 'tun'. This suffix, preceded by the settler's name, might well be adopted as the name for the new settlement. Ednaston, for instance, is simply 'Ednoth's tun'; Wednesbury is 'Woden's hill' to commemorate the Germanic god. Unfortunately, we cannot find a place name that can be readily associated with the Eldreds. Not, that is, in England: in the United States there are townships named Eldred to commemorate settlers from the Old Country.

English county boundaries had changed little until quite recently since they were drawn in Saxon times. The framework of the English legal system is Saxon, despite the fact that the very word 'law' is not Saxon but Danish! This is one of the many curiosities arising out of the mix of Saxon and Dane. At first bitter enemies, they eventually learned to live together peaceably; by the time of the Norman Conquest the two races had fused into one nation.

Most of the customs passed down to us from our Saxon forbears seem to relate to eating and drinking. Perhaps this is because feasting, after fighting and farming, stood high among their most cherished activities. Picture the great hall of a lord's house, with all the guests seated around a long trestle table, their shields and weapons hung from a beam above them, eating with a knife. Only the rich owned spoons and forks, and even they used a knife at the table. Table glass, like the clothes they wore, was colourful, decorated with hollow gouts of molten glass into which the wine could flow. Many drinking glasses had no feet to stand on, which suggests that the contents would be tossed off at a draught and the vessel replenished from a pottery urn. The hall was lit by candles, rush lights or oil lamps. At New Year celebrations the custom was to salute one another over a cup of spiced ale. This came to be known as the wassail bowl because the Saxons, in bidding you good health, cried 'Waes Heil!'. After the introduction of Christianity it became known as the 'loving cup', which is the centre of a charming ceremony dating from Saxon times. The custom is observed on special occasions at College and City of London banquets, and derives from an incident at a feast in 978 when the Saxon king, Edward the Martyr, was treacherously slain while drinking a stoup of wine. Today the loving cup is a silver bowl with two handles, a napkin being tied to one of them. Two persons stand, one to drink and the other to defend the drinker. After he has taken his draught, the drinker wipes the cup with the napkin and passes it to the defender. The next person rises to defend the new drinker, and so on around the table. The Yule (or Ewell) log and the practice of decorating our houses with evergreens at Christmas are other customs which we owe to our Saxon ancestors.

****

'The name is Saxon, so that the family, as justly as some others, may claim to have subsisted even before the Norman Conquest'. Thus wrote the 18th-century historian, the Rev. Philip Morant, of the Eldreds of Olivers, near Colchester in Essex. Morant was well qualified to comment: he was editor of the first records of the British

Parliament and author of a survey of Essex. The editor of *Burke's Armoury* supports Morant's view. 'The Eldreds', he writes, 'are descended from a very ancient family, claiming Saxon origin'.

For more than 1,000 years the Eldreds, as members of a race of great travellers and colonisers, have spread throughout the Anglo-Saxon world, and beyond. The family is particularly well-established in the United States, Canada and Australia, and there are Eldrids (spelt with an 'i') of British origin living in Argentina. Etymologists believe that the wide range of variations in the spelling of 'Eldred' all relate to the same family. These include, among others, Aldread, Aldritt, Aldred, Eldrid, Eldritt, Elldread. People spelled by ear rather than by rule before the standardisation of spelling in the 17th and 18th centuries. Shakespeare used more than one version of his own name, as can be seen from his signatures.

Perhaps the two most common versions of 'Eldred' that appear in the chronicles of Saxon England are 'Ealdred' and 'Aedelred'. The first means 'old counsel', much as 'ealdorman' or 'alderman', and signifies an elder or senior man. Until recently Old Street, in the city of London, was also known as Eald Street. The second version means 'noble counsel'. The prefix 'Aedel' corresponds to the modern German word 'edel' meaning noble, which appears in the name of the Alpine plant edelweiss. It is not surprising that there is a link between Anglo-Saxon and German, as our Saxon ancestors originally came from north-west Germany. Their close neighbours were two similar Teutonic peoples with whom they shared a common language and a common culture: the Angles, from the area where Germany meets Denmark, and the Jutes, who came from Friesland and the Rhineland. As related earlier, all three tribes began to invade England in the middle of the fifth century when it was still under Roman rule.

* * * * *

How did the Eldred family fit into the troubled background of Saxon England? The name, in one of its variations, appears in documents of the period, including Domesday Book. This indicates that then, as later, there were Eldreds in many areas of the country, and that they fulfilled various roles in the social hierarchy from king down. Here are a few biographical details about the most prominent of them in descending order of importance.

King Edred, or Eadred, as his name is spelt on the foundation under the traditional Saxon coronation stone at Kingston in Surrey, was a great-grandson of Alfred the Great. He ascended the throne in 946, but suffered from chronic ill health and died in 955 in his early thirties. He appears to have fought his illness bravely and on the whole he was a successful, though hard-fisted, ruler who in 952 slaughtered the people of Thetford in Norfolk for killing an abbot. In dealings with the Danes he showed courage and resolve. He left lavish sums of money to the Church and to the English people, with the exception of the Northumbrians who had tried unsuccessfully to rise against his authority. Like his father, Edward the Elder, Edred was thoughtful in leaving money for the relief of famine and, if necessary, to buy off an enemy army. As noted earlier, his chief minister was Archbishop Dunstan. King

Edred is buried in Winchester Cathedral. There was once a wharf in the City of London, near St Paul's Cathedral, called Eadred's Hythe. It was one of the principal quays on the Thames, and foreign vessels discharged their cargoes there in Saxon times. Whether it was named after the king is not known; it later became known as Queen Hythe.

Next in importance is Aldred, or Ealdred, Archbishop of York, who held high office at a milestone in history, playing a leading role in the drama of 1066 and the succession of William of Normandy to the throne of England. We first read of him when he was Bishop of Worcester in the reign of Edward the Confessor. He visited Cologne for about a year on a mission for the king, and was received with great ceremony. No reason for his visit was given by the compiler of the *Anglo-Saxon Chronicle*, but it would seem likely that it had to do with the choice of a successor for the English king who had no heir. After William the Conqueror's victory in 1066, Aldred, then Archbishop of York, joined a group of 'all the best men from London' who submitted to William at Berkhampstead, 'from force of circumstance, when the depredation was complete'. They gave William hostages and in return he promised to be a 'gracious lord' to them. Aldred performed the coronation service for William on Christmas Day 1066 in the great new church of St Peter's at Westminster. As related earlier, Stigand, Archbishop of Canterbury, would normally have crowned the new king; He was, however, out of favour with William, and was allowed only to assist at the service in his role as Bishop of Winchester. Aldred died in 1069.

An Ealdred was High Reeve of Bamburgh and Earldorman (or Earl) of Northumbria. He was defeated in battle by the Viking Raegnald in 915. Ealdred was one of the northern rulers in 920 who recognized the overlordship of Edward the Elder, father of King Edred.

Moving down the social scale, we find references to other Eldreds as landowners of varying degree. There is, for instance, record of a grant of land by King Athelstan to his thane, Ealdread, in Chalgrove, Bedfordshire. Another Ealdread, a thane of Edward the Confessor, owned land in Hertfordshire, which after the Norman Conquest was granted to the Bishop of London.

Chronicles have recorded only some of the men of the Eldred family who played a part in the making of England's history. What of the rest – the men and women who lived out their lives in such humble circumstances that there was no one to record their modest achievements for posterity? Nevertheless, let us not forget them. What more fitting memorial than these verses from Gray's *Elegy*?

> Oft did the harvest to their sickle yield,
> Their furrow oft the stubborn glebe has broke:
> How jocund did they drive their team afield!
> How bow'd the woods beneath their sturdy stroke;
>
> Let not ambition mock their useful toil,
> Their homely joys and destiny obscure;
> Nor grandeur hear with a disdainful smile
> The short and simple annals of the poor.

Chapter Three

Eldred Coats of Arms

The record of Eldred coats of arms is a long and interesting one. The original is one of a comparatively small number used by right of long service rather than by right of a royal 'grant'. Existing records and references indicate that the armorial bearings of Eldred were established as the family 'badge' more than 600 years ago and that it is one of the oldest Saxon coats. Unfortunately, there is no record or tradition to trace its origin and, therefore, it is not possible to determine the precise time that it came into being.

A family coat of arms was an important social matter several hundred years ago. Today much of the significance has been lost, and only a few people know much about heraldry or the science of designing and interpreting coats of arms. Nevertheless it is still a fascinating subject and those whose ancestry entitles them to bear arms can be justly proud of the fact.

Insecurity was universal in medieval times and many disputes were settled by force. Formal education was rare and only a few of the most prominent and wealthy could read and write. It became an accepted practice to use a distinctive 'badge' for identification. The device could be displayed publicly as a banner or flag, or engraved on metal to form a 'seal'. A knight in armour was totally camouflaged and his personal badge was his only means of identification. This would be emblazoned on the trappings of his horse, painted on his shield, or molded on to the top of his helmet as a 'crest'. Eventually these devices were combined into an ornate 'achievement', called a coat of arms, as it was often embroidered on the cape or coat which the knight wore over his armour.

A coat of arms was the exclusive property of the family it represented, and it was dishonourable to use the 'achievement' belonging to someone else. Initially, each eligible individual had his own crest that was regarded as part of the whole coat of arms; in later years, the same crest was used by members of a family. A 'motto', the battle cry or expression of the principal owner, was placed usually within a scroll above the crest, or below the escutcheon (shield).

The custom of using a coat of arms was introduced in Europe during the Crusades. At first, the symbols used on the arms were selected by the owner and represented an important incident or quality in his life. As duplication of symbols and designs resulted from lack of a system to monitor the usage of armorial bearings, King Richard III of England established the Heralds' College (College of Arms) in London in 1484 to bring order out of confusion. The college was given full authority to control and supervise matters of entitlement, design, and the use of coats of arms. The official in charge was called a Herald with the title of 'King at Arms of Englishmen'. The king issued a decree that all coat armour used without the authorisation of the King's Herald was 'spurious' (without legal sanction), thereby reserving to himself the right to decide who should and should not bear arms.

A violent argument arose at once. Those whose family coat of arms had been used for many years – hundreds of years in some cases – claimed that authority should not rest entirely with the king. They contended that lineal descendants of families that had used armorial bearings for a long time should be entitled to continue the usage. The argument was settled by permitting the Herald to 'confirm' or 'exemplify' a person in the use of his arms if he could prove lineal descent for 100 years or more in a family that had been using the arms during that time. Persons in this category had 'right of use by prescription', whereas those who did not meet this requirement were granted the 'right of use by grant of the King's Herald'.

The Herald made 'visitations' to counties throughout England at irregular intervals during the period 1530-1688. He required persons using arms to prove their right to use them and granted new coats to those who were eligible. The Herald also supervised tournaments and trials by combat, recorded deeds of chivalry, and arbitrated matters on armorial bearings. The discharge of his many duties eventually became a complicated science with laws, customs, regulations and even its own nomenclature. The College of Arms still operates in London, housed in a splendid old building in Queen Victoria Street near St Paul's Cathedral.

Glossary of Terms
Some basic heraldic terms and definitions have been selected to help the reader to understand the technical description of the various Eldred coats of arms that are included in this assemblage.

All proper	In natural colours.
Base	Lower third of a shield.
Base Point	Lower centre portion of a shield.
Bend Raguly	A bend, bar or similar device with serrated edges like saw teeth. Probably a later version of bend trunked.
Bend Trunked	A bend in the form of a tree trunk with the branches lopped off close to the trunk. The tree is cut off at the top and separated from the root.
Bezant	A golden or yellow roundel, disk, or coin of Byzantium; signifies wealth.
Bird	Numerous species of birds are used in heraldic art, e.g. the Roman eagle and the German eagle. British heraldry used a lion more often than a bird.
Blazon	Technical description of arms using heraldic language.

Charge	A device, geometrical pattern or pictorial character; e.g. the lion, eagle, star, and leopard.
Chief	Upper third of a shield.
Coat of arms	A heraldic design consisting of a shield, crest and motto. Originally a surcoat embroidered with one's family escutcheon. Later, the escutcheon of a family or person, armorial bearings, or device symbolic of ranks and deeds.

Colours:

Azure	Blue; loyalty and truth.
Gules	Red; military fortitude and magnanimity.
Purpure	Purple; royal majesty, sovereignty and justice.
Sable	Black; shown by cross-hatched and horizontal lines.
Vert	Green; hope, joy, loyalty and love.

Crest	A heraldic device placed above the shield; originally a special mark of honour.
Cross	Many different varieties, each with a specific name, are used in heraldic art.
Dexter	Bearer's right (observer's left) hand.
Difference	Additional device to show family relationship (Cadency mark) (marks of cadency), i.e. the mullet – mark of third son; the martlet – mark of fourth son; the fleur-de-lis – mark of sixth son; and others.
Erect	Standing on end, instead of horizontal.
Escutcheon	A surface, usually shield, shaped for displaying armorial bearings; viewed as though borne by a person facing the observer.
Fesse	Center third of a shield.
Fur	Substituted in place of tinctures, e.g.. ermine and vair.
Lion (or leopard)	A heraldic animal that is found frequently in heraldic art. There are many different shapes, sizes and colours.

Metals:

Argent	Silver; peace and sincerity.
Or	Gold, or yellow; generosity and elevation of mind.
Motto	Expression of one's guiding principal; battle cry of the owner in early times.
Per Bend	A band diagonally from dexter (observer's upper left) to sinister (observer's lower right), properly one third of the width, but often less.
Per Fess	Straight line dividing the shield horizontally.
Per Pale	Straight line dividing the shield perpendicularly.
Ragged Staff	Symbolic of the huge club that folklore giants carried.
Sinister	Bearer's left (observer's right) hand.
Tinctures	Colours applied to the shield, representing metals, colours proper, and various furs.
Trick	Sketch; drawing that shows the tinctures in a coat of arms.
Wreath	A narrow band with six twists, formed of the two chief colours (tinctures) in the arms. The metal is the first twist on the dexter side.

Eldred Coat Armour in England

The Eldred family, including various spellings of the name, is descended from the Saxons. Some genealogical researchers believe that there is an ancestral connection to the Saxon royal line in England. This belief is based on King Eadred (Edred), who was the Saxon king from 946-55. The validity of this descent has not yet been proven, but as the earliest record of an 'Eldred' coat of arms (pre-heraldic period) is one credited to Eadred, we are including herewith its description, sketch and background material.

Eadred (Edred), King of England 946-55 A.D.

Arms: Blazoned Azure, a cross forming between four martlets or.

King Eadred was the son of King
Edward (reigned 901-25); grandson of
King Alfred the Great (reigned 871-
99); great-grandson of King Ethelwulf
(reigned 839-57); and great-great-
grandson of King Egbert (called first
King of all England, born *c*.775,
crowned King of the West Saxons in
802, overlord of all English kings in
829, died in 839).

Eadred was the second of the six
boy kings:
1. Edmund I, Magnificus, reign
940-46.
2. Eadred (Edred, Ealdred), reign
946-55 (Edmund's brother).
3. Edwig (Edwy), reign 955-59
(Edmund's son).
4. Edgar the Peaceful, reign 959-75
(Edwig's brother).
5. Edward the Martyr, reign 975-78
(Edgar's son).
6. Ethelred, reign 978-1016 (Edgar's
son).
These six Saxon kings were followed
by Edmund II, Ironside (reign April
1016 – November 1016). The reigns of
these men were short; their corona-
tions took place in Kingston-on-
Thames and the original Saxon coronation stone survives today outside the
Guildhall. When Edmund II died after
only seven months on the English

1. Coronation stone of King Eadred outside the
Guildhall, Kingston upon Thames.

throne, Canute (or Cnut) the Dane (*c*.994-1035) became King of England (1016)
and King of Denmark (1019).

Eadred was raised by his sister Ae̱thelflaed and her husband Ae̱thelraed. King
Edmund left male issue but as they were very young when he died his brother
Eadred was selected to be king. His responsibilities as a ruler included being King of
Wessex, Mercia, Northumbria, the Britons of Cornwall, the Anglo-Saxons of the
Danelaw, and of the Norse, Danes and English around York. During his nine-year
reign, Eadred's armies fought and conquered the Northmen – the Danes and the
Norwegians (Sea-Kings). According to history, Eadred was a superstitious person and
his actions were guided largely by Dunstan, Abbot of Glastonbury.

Dunstan became his councillor in major governmental matters and head of the
treasury. From this strong position, Dunstan was able to promote his ecclesiastical
views and policies throughout the kingdom. Serious differences arose between the

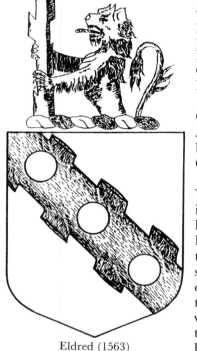

Eldred (1563)

monks and the secular clergy, resulting in theological confusion which caused much agitation among the people. The monks, supported by Dunstan, were powerful during Eadred's nine-year reign, but were less so after his death. Eadred is buried in Winchester Cathedral. As he left only young children, his nephew, Edwy, was chosen to succeed him.

Original Eldred Arms per the King's Herald, 1563
Arms: Or, on a bend gules trunked sable, three bezants.
Crest: A demi-lion supporting a ragged staff, erect.

The first mention of an Eldred coat of arms that is still in use is the record made by the King's Herald during his 'visitation' to Norfolk in 1563 and recorded in the Herald's *'Booke of Norfolk'*. Since the original records of this visit have been lost, there is no absolute proof showing that this first official recognition was a 'grant' or 'confirmation'. However, the Herald 'confirmed' the arms to John Eldred of Great Saxham in 1592 by virtue of his descent through the Norfolk Eldreds. In this respect, John proved that the arms he claimed had been used rightfully by his great-great-grandfather Nicholas Eldred (*bef.* 1454-*c.*1514). Acceptance of this proof by the Herald meant evidence was submitted showing continuous use of the arms by the Eldred family for a hundred years or more before Nicholas' time.

This shield was gold; there was a tree trunk in red with its branches cut off close to the trunk and with the bark and branch stubs inserted or outlined in black. The butt of the tree trunk was in the lower right hand quarter of the shield and the top on the upper left quarter. This particular diagonal trunk was very popular in the early days of heraldry, signifying strength and power. The 'bezant' was a golden disk depicting money or wealth.

The Eldred family crest was confirmed by the King's Herald as belonging exclusively to the Eldred family during his 'visit' to the county of Norfolk, England, in 1563. The description reveals a demi-lion sitting on its haunches; the demi-lion's body from the hips down is 'couped' (missing). A demi-lion was a purely imaginative heraldic device, highly formalised in character and only remotely connected with an actual lion. This imaginary animal is holding a tree trunk 'device' upright in his paws; a plain wreath is underneath the demi-lion and trunk.

Sometimes the Herald specified colours or other details about a crest; in other cases, he left the colour combination up to the owner. It was customary, however, to reverse the colours of the shield in the crest. The original Eldred crest was probably a golden demi-lion holding a red tree trunk. Other colour combinations have included a golden lion and a sable staff, and occasionally a red lion and a sable staff.

The Herald seldom specified a motto as it was not considered an important part of the coat of arms. One prominent genealogist who made an extensive study of the Eldred arms believed that the original arms had a motto – 'Nunc aut Nunquam', meaning 'Now or Never'. Another one believed the motto was 'Vincet que se Vincet', meaning 'He who conquers himself, conquers'. Others that can be seen include 'Mente Manque', meaning 'Mind and Hand' (Sir Revett Eldred), 'Industria et Spee', meaning 'By Industry and Hope' (John Eldred of Olivers), and 'By the Name of Eldred', displayed on the arms painted by William Coles for Keziah Eldred Nye in 1796.

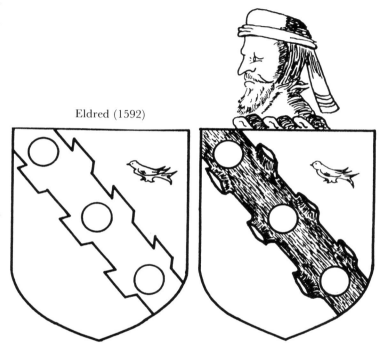

Eldred (1592)

John Eldred (1556-1632) 'The Traveller', London and Great Saxham, Suffolk, England

Arms: The shield gold on a bend gules trunked sable, three bezants. A martlet gules for his difference.

Crest: Upon a wreath of his colours an Arabian's head proper bearded and coyffed sable tyed about with a band and the pendant argent, the ends gemmely and fringed gules.

John Eldred, 'The Traveller', was the fourth son of John Eldred of Buckenham, Norfolk. His grandfather was John Eldred of Knettishall; his great-grandfather William Eldred of Knettishall; and his great-great-grandfather Nicholas Eldred (*bef.* 1454-*c.*1514) of Knettishall; and his great-great-great-grandfather John Eldred (*bef.* 1419-89) of Corby, Lincolnshire (now Corby Glen).

In all probability, John Eldred had been using his arms for some time before the Herald's 'visitation' to Suffolk in 1592 and had so notified that official. The confirmation on file among the rolls of the College of Arms is the oldest existing document on the Eldred arms:

'ELDRED'

TO ALL AND SINGULAR WHOM IT MAY CONCERN know by these presents that I WILLIAM DETHICK als garter Principal King at Arms of Englishmen, being by credible report informed that John ELDRED of London and Great Saxham in Suffolk, gentle-

man, the fourthe sonne of John Eldred of Buckenham, sonne of John Eldred of Knet-
sell in the Countie of Norfolke, gentleman, who also is descended out of auntient linage
and parentage of good credit and abilitie and being requested to make declaration and
testimonie for his Armes as may best agree with the records and profe shewed in my
Office, I the said Garter Principall King-at-Arms of Englishmen, by these doe signifie
and declare, conferme, blazen and exemplefie this shield or Coat of Armes to the said
John ELDRED and to his posteritie lawfully begotten to be by him and to them borne
with their due difference according to the Lawes of Armes forever, viz,

The shield gold on a Bend Gules
trunked Sables Three Bezants.
A martlet Gules for his difference

      And for his further augmentation I have GRANTED unto him upon his Best and
Commendable deserts and travailes especially in Arabia where hee lived seven yeares for
his Crest or Cognizance

Upon a Wreathe of his Collours an
Arabians head proper bearded and
Coyyfed Sable and Tyed about wth
a Band and the Pendant Argent the
ends Gemmely and fringed gules.

      In WITNESS WHEREOF I have unto these Presents affexed the seale of mine
Office and subscribed my name, Done and dated in Office of Armes, London, 10 June,
34 Elizabeth, A.D. 1592.

(signed) WILLIAM DETHICK
Garter, Principall King at
Armes of Englishmen.

John Eldred used these arms for 40 years until his death in 1632, and they may be
seen on many documents of his time. There are some drawings of his arms that the
King's Herald, however, specified 'bend gules trunked sable', and there is no official
document to support 'bend raguly'.

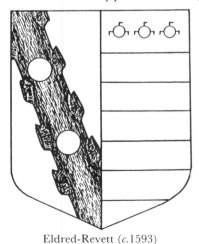

Eldred-Revett (*c.*1593)

Eldred-Revett coat of arms, Suffolk, England
Arms: Party per pale or, a bend trunked sables, a
martlet in sinister chief, for Eldred argent, three bars
sable, per chief, three trivits of the last for Revett.

John Eldred used this coat of arms when he wished to
give recognition to both his own and his wife's family.
His wife, Mary Revett (Revit, Rivet, Rivett) whom he
married in 1593 after his journey to Arabia, came of
an armour bearing family. John combined her family
arms with his to form the 'Eldred-Revett' coat of arms.
This action was permitted by the laws of heraldry and
employed a method called 'impaling', or 'party per

pale'. The shield was divided in half vertically with the left half used to display the husband's arms and the right half for the wife's arms. Since the two coats were recorded already, there was no need to record the combined arms. The 'trivit' mentioned in the description of his wife's arms is a heraldic device of purely imaginary origin, rhyming with 'Revett'.

John Eldred (1565-1646), Olivers, Stanway, Colchester, Essex, England

Arms: Azure, a cross pattée fitchèe or, on a chief of the last three globes of the first.
Crest: A triton proper bearing in hands an escallop or.
Motto: Industria et Spee

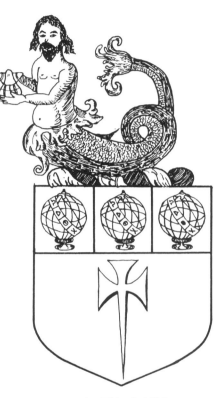

The first Eldred to patent a coat of arms radically different from the original coat of the Norfolk Eldreds was John Eldred, a son of Thomas Eldred of Ipswich, Suffolk and a descendant of John Eldred of Corby, Lincolnshire, a user of the Eldred arms. Like his father, John of Olivers, (the name of his country estate), was a merchant at Colchester in Essex. He was a Justice of the Peace, a member of Parliament, Alderman, Mayor of the town and owner of two houses. Rather than prove his right to use the Eldred arms, he obtained a coat of arms in 1630 that was quite different from any on record.

The basis of John Eldred's achievement was his father's exploit of sailing around the world with Thomas Cavendish in 1586-88. He was a frequent visitor to London and probably went directly to the College of Arms with his request, as Essex was not visited by the King's Herald until 1634. The wording of his 'grant' is somewhat different from John of Great Saxham's 'confirmation'.

John Eldred, 1630

'ELDRED'

TO ALL AND SINGULAR UNTO WHOM THESE PRESENTS SHALL COME Sir Richard St George, Clarinceaux, King-at-Arms of Englishmen, sendeth greetings.

WHEREAS John Eldred of Colchester in the County of Essex, son of Thomas Eldred of Ipswich, Suffolk, son of Nicholas Eldred of New Buckenham, Norfolk, gentleman, hath desired me to assign unto him such Arms as he and his lawful prosperity may bear.

KNOW YE THEREFORE that I have saw fit to assign unto him the armes hereunder mentioned, vizt.,

Azure, a cross pattée fitchèe or,
on a chief of the last three globes
azure.

which armes, I, the said Sir Richard St George, garter, Clarinceaux, King-at-arms of Englishmen, by these presents do signify, blazon, and declare and GRANT unto the said John ELDRED of Colchester and by the authority granted unto me by the Letters Patent of my said Office made unto me under the Great Seal of England do give and assign the saide John Eldred and to his posterity lawfully begotten by him, to be by him and by them borne with their due differences according to the Laws of Armes forever in witness whereof I have affixed the seal of mine Office and set my hand, dated in the Office of Armes at London, Feb. the 14th, A.D. 1630.

(signed) Sir Richard St George
garter, King-at-Arms of Englishmen.

In a separate grant, the Herald assigned a crest: 'A triton proper bearing in hands an escallop, or'; the motto reads 'Industria et Spee', meaning 'By Industry and Hope'. The whole theme of these arms is nautical, and the inspiration must have come from the exploits of John's father: the blue of the shield is the blue of the sea, 'triton' is a heraldic term for merman, and an 'escallop' is the heraldic sea-shell. The three globes suggest the world around which his father sailed; the only resemblance to the old Eldred arms is the number of globes – three – the same number as the 'bezants', and the gold on part of the shield. This coat of arms was used by John of Olivers and his heirs for almost 150 years, when male heirs failed and the arms became extinct.

Peter Eldred (d.1642), 'Citizen and Grocer of Broad Street', London

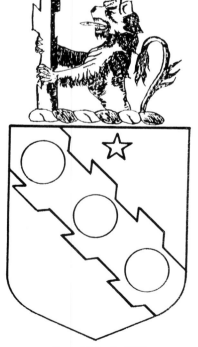

Peter Eldred, 1633

The meaning of the word 'grocery' in the 17th century was quite different from its modern usage. It referred to the fact that members of the Grocers Guild or Company sold goods, mainly spices, drugs and tobacco *en gros* or wholesale. The Grocers were the second in seniority of the 12 Great Companies of the City, a position they retain today.

Arms: Or, on a band gules trunked sable, three bezants. A mullett gules per chief for a difference.

Crest: A demi-lion or, holding in paws a ragged staff sable, erect.

John Eldred of Great Saxham had an older brother named Peter who had a son named Peter. This younger Peter Eldred, who belonged to the Grocers Company, had evidently been using the old family arms. When the King's Herald 'visited' London in the winter of 1633-34, he notified Peter to appear before him and show 'profe' that he was using his arms with proper authority. Peter had plenty of proof; he only had to prove descent from his grandfather since John Eldred of Great Saxham had already proved descent far enough back to secure 'confirmation'.

The Herald confirmed Peter's use of his arms and use of the family crest. He sketched the arms and crest on the margin of the confirmation, stating that they were 'vide the Booke of Norfolke' made 70 years before. Although the Herald described the bend as 'gules trunked sable', he sketched it as 'bend raguly'. The mullet on the shield is a 5-pointed star, which signified that Peter was a third son, as was his father. The coat armour of Peter 'The Grocer' and John of Great Saxham are the only coats the Herald ever confirmed and are the only existing blazons of the original Eldred arms.

John Eldred (1638-1719), Barrister, London /Oxford/ Kent, England

Arms: Or, a bend gules raguly sable; in dexter base point a mullet gules for a difference.

Peter Eldred, the Grocer, died in 1642, and left a son named John – a third son as were his father and grandfather. During John's student days at St John's College, Oxford (he graduated with an M.A. degree in 1661) he began to use a coat of arms, evidently without registering it at the College of Arms. This coat was based on his father's coat, and therefore he had a right to use it. John became a barrister in Ashurst, Kent.

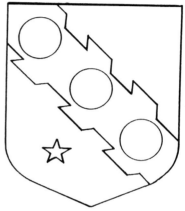

John Eldred, *c.*1654

Sir Revett Eldred (1591-1652), Baronetcy created 29 January 1641, London and Great Saxham, England

Arms: Or, a bend raguly sable, bearing three bezants.
Crest: A dexter hand, couped, fessways, reaching to a laurel crown, all proper.
Motto: Mente Manque.

Each son of John Eldred of Great Saxham had the heraldic right to use his father's coat of arms, with the proper 'difference' shown on the shield. His eldest son, Revett, used these arms prior to his father's death in 1632; the blazon was 'Or, on a bend gules trunked sable, three bezants; per chief a martlet gules; a label in dexter base point for difference'. This label (difference mark) was probably gules.

Revett and his wife Anne lived most of their lives in London, spending less and less time at Great Saxham after his father's death. They became engrossed in the political and social life of the capital city, and this led to a desire for a baronetcy. None of the Eldreds had ever been so honoured. Even the prominent John Eldred of Great Saxham was never knighted. At the time, a good way to achieve the honour was to patent a coat of arms. In 1642, Revett secured a 'grant' of arms and was knighted the same year – the only Eldred to receive a title.

The grant was made to 'Revett Eldred of Great Saxham and London' before he was knighted. His shield was gold, and there was an up-to-date form of the old 'trunked' bend in black with three bezants. Evidently, he wanted to retain an image of the original Eldred arms, for he could rightly be proud of its ancient heritage as

Sir Revett Eldred, 1641

one of the very few coats of Saxon origin. The crest he chose was new: a right hand cut off at the wrist, palm to the front, stretching toward a laurel crown just out of reach, all in natural colours.

James I of England (James Stuart, King James VI of Scotland) distributed knighthoods freely among his subjects to raise money:

> Some of them tried to decline the honour; but James pushed through a law that knighthood could be enforced, under penalty of a heavy fine, on anyone worth more than £40 a year. In May 1611 the king also created the new title of baronet in order to raise money, by selling it for the considerable sum of £1,095. But so many of the titles were made available that the price fell to £200.

Every Eldred coat of arms after Sir Revett's patent, except for his widow's, followed its general design. In fact, the 'bend raguly sable' became so identified with the Eldred arms that many do not realise that this design was not the blazon of the original coat. There are lists of coat armour of both John Eldred of Great Saxham and Peter Eldred, the Grocer, as having a 'bend raguly sable', but there is no official record to warrant this description.

Several of the Norfolk Eldreds used coat armour patterned after Sir Revett's during the latter part of the 17th century. Since a grant cannot be found for these arms, their use was seemingly without heraldic sanction. By this time, however, it was quite safe for any member of the Eldred family to use the arms. Many descriptions had been recorded from an observed use and, therefore, one could not attribute a specific design to a particular family.

Joseph Eldred (1609-45), L.L.B. Frithwood, Fellow of New College, Oxford, England
Arms: 1. (Prior to 1641). Or, a bend raguly sable bearing three bezants, a martlet gules beaked sable in dexter base point for a difference.
2. (1641). Or, a bend raguly sable, per chief a martlet gules beaked sable.
Crest: Out of a ducal coronet, a peacock's tail, ppr.

Joseph Eldred (a.k.a. Eldridge and Eldrige), the youngest son of John Eldred of Great Saxham, was a bachelor who was studiously inclined throughout his life

(Fellow of New College, Oxford). He died in 1645 and was buried in College Chapel. Where his brother, Revett, was using arms, Joseph was using coat armour also. His use of arms made it necessary for both of them to have a 'difference' (martlet) on some or other part of the shield to avoid confusion.

Joseph introduced a radical change into the design of the Eldred coat of arms. In place of the 'bend trunked sable', he used the 'bend raguly' – a change from the lopped-off trunk stubs to serrated sawlike edges. He changed from the two colours of red and black

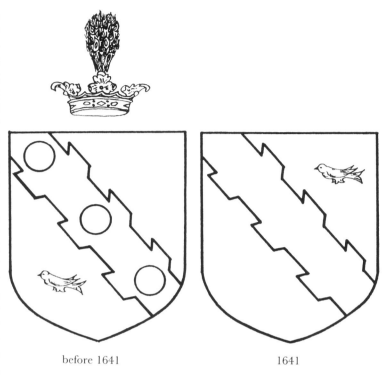

before 1641   1641

on the bend trunked sable to black – the authorised colour on a bend raguly. The colour gules (red) was dropped, except for use in the difference; the martlet on Joseph's arms had a black beak.

The grant of arms in 1641 to Revett Eldred literally took the heart out of the arms that Joseph was using. Being the eldest son, Revett simply took Joseph's coat from him and forced Joseph to get another one. His new arms were 'Or, a bend raguly sable, per chief a martlet gules beaked sable'. Thus he retained the shield and the bend raguly sable; the martlet was his by right of birth.

Anne, Lady Eldred (d.1671), Relict of Sir Revett Eldred, London, England

Arms: Gules, on a chevron argent three leopards' heads between quarterfoyles of the first.

The only grant of arms to a woman under the Eldred name was made to Anne, Lady Eldred after her husband's death. Under the Law of Arms there were certain restrictions imposed on women who desired to 'bear arms'. They were not permitted to 'wear' either the crest or motto; under certain conditions, they were not allowed to use the shield for a field, but instead used a diamond shaped field called a 'lozenge'. Anne, Lady did not inherit the right to bear her husband's arms; however, since she 'held court' regularly at Great Saxham after his death, she had a social use for arms and asked for a new coat.

Anne, Lady Eldred, 1652

Her 'achievement' was entirely different from any other Eldred coat of arms that had ever been devised. The idea, or inspiration, behind her design is unknown, but it is believed that the leopards' heads had at least a remote relationship and symbolism. The original grant was issued on 6 December 1652:

'ELDRED'

TO ALL AND SINGULAR UNTO WHOME THESE PRESENTS SHALL COME, Edward BYSSHE, Esq., Garter, Principal Kinge of Armes of Englishmen, sendeth greetinge.
WHEREAS Mrs. Anne Eldred, the relict of Sir Revett ELDRED, late of Great Saxham in the County of Suffolk, Esqre, and one of the daughters of John Blaikway of Hornidge in the County of Salop, hath desired me to assign unto her such armes as she and her postertie may lawfullie beare.
KNOW YE THEREFORE that I thought fit to assigne unto her the Armes hereunder mentioned, viz.

> Gules, on a chevron argent three
> leopards' heads between three
> quarterfoyles of the first, as
> they are depicted in the margin,

which Armes I, the said Edward BYSSHE, Garter, Principal Kinge at Armes of Englishmen, by authoritie granted unto me by the letters patent of my said office made unto me under the GREAT SEAL OF ENGLAND, doe by these presents assign, give and grant unto the said Mrs. Anne ELDRED, and her posteritie lawfullie begotten by her, arms borne with their due difference according to the Lawes of Armes forever. In witness whereof I have unto these presents affixed the Seal of mine office and subscribed by name.

Dated at the Office of Armes in London, the sixth day of December in the year of Our Lord one thousand six hundred and fiftie two.

(Signed) E. BYSSHE
Garter, Principal, Kinge of Armes
of Englishmen

The blazon means 'on a red background is a white (or silver) chevron, upon which, arranged alternately, are three leopards' heads outlined in black and three red four-leaf clovers'. A 'quarterfoyle' is a heraldic device much like a four-leaf clover, and the word 'first' refers to the first colour mentioned, namely gules (red). The first left-hand 'charge' is a leopard's head since it is first mentioned; the last at the right would be a 'quarterfoyle'; and the chevron has the angle pointing up. There was no crest or motto as women could not bear them.

This is the last Eldred coat of arms recorded at the College of Arms.

Eldred Coat Armour in America

Many of the wealthy landowners in England, who called themselves country 'gentlemen', had arms. Although heraldry is concerned with family lineage, the authorised possession of arms became synonymous with the upper class. Since most of the ancestors of colonial families did not come from this group, they were inclined to deride the use of coat armour as snobbery. After the Revolution, however, many Americans took delight in flaunting in the face of 'blue-blood' Americans and upper-class Englishmen the fact that the use of arms and family crests in America did not imply an exclusive prerogative of a privileged class. It was a right belonging to anyone who declared his descent from a person whose use of arms had been authorised by an ancient heraldic action.

It became a fad to display a coat of arms or family crest, especially during the period 1790-1825. Wandering heraldic artists thrived all over the country, especially in the Northern States, painting coats of arms for anyone who would pay the price. Since many Americans of English origin could claim ancestral arms from one of the hundreds on record, the artist could easily find and paint the coat armour of any family that had one recorded. The client was not versed in the law of arms, and the artist was painting to make money. This combination resulted in a flourishing business, with prices ranging from $10 to $50. Regardless of the degree of artistic success, the finished products were indignantly scorned by heraldic circles in England. The American user, however, did not care about heraldic details and displayed his arms as he pleased. These coats of arms were used widely for 25 years as decorations on carriages, china, furniture and as architectural ornaments. Hundreds were painted and placed in picture frames for hanging on the wall, and many Americans still have them as cherished family heirlooms.

One of the last, and best, American heraldic artists was John William Coles, or William Coles as he most frequently signed his name. He worked in the region around Boston during 1795-1820 and learned the art from his father, John Coles Sr. It is often difficult to distinguish the work of one from the other. The general pattern of both 'achievements' was very much alike, but the details varied. William Coles almost always used some form of motto, while his father seldom did. Both used a decoration on either side at the bottom of their coats which they called 'palm leaves', but which are much more like cornstalks. William invariably folded one leaf of these palms, usually the left one, in between two other leaves. The top of the shield was three-

Eldred arms by 'William Cole, Heraldry Painter, Boston, Febr'y 1796'

lobed, but William made his more uniform. The work, when compared with a first-class heraldic artist's, was crude and lacking in much of the detailed exactness demanded by heraldic disciples.

In 1795, Colonel David Nye of North Falmouth, Massachusetts, married as his second wife, Keziah Eldred, a descendant of William[1] Eldred of Yarmouth. Perhaps influenced by the fad of the times, Colonel Nye had an Eldred coat of arms painted to please his wife. On the back of the painting was this description:

'ELDRED'

He beareth, – Or, a bend sable charged with three bezants, raguled, in base a martlet gules, beaked sable. Was the coat of Joseph Eldred, L.L.B. and Fellow in New College, Oxford, Anno Dom – 1645.

True Copy from Heraldry
William Coles
Heraldry Painter
Boston
Feb'r'y 1796

This coat of arms, painted by Coles, was not in fact a true copy from heraldry. The martlet is placed in sinister chief, as it appears in the coat armour of John Eldred of Great Saxham, instead of his son Joseph, as the blazon reads. Perhaps Keziah liked the 'bird' in the upper part of the shield better than the lower, so Coles put it there. The artists of the time had no reluctance in taking liberties with heraldic customs in that fashion.

Colonel Potiphar (Potter) Eldred, a descendant of Samuel[1] Eldred of Massachusetts and Rhode Island, also had a coat of arms painted. His description reads:

It was about two feet long and one and a quarter wide, painted in oils on canvas and framed with a black walnut frame. It was a gold shield with a grey background. There was a broad black band having edges somewhat like the teeth of a saw extending from the upper left corner of the shield to the lower right corner. At the top, just above the shield and extending nearly to the edges, was what looked like a cord twisted from two threads, one black and one yellow. On it was a yellow lion rampant resting his paws against a part of a tree trunk in black and gray. Underneath was the name 'ELDRED'. There were no fancy streamers such as I have seen in pictures of coats of arms.

There are other instances recorded of Eldred coats of arms in America, but the preceding examples are considered a basic pattern of those that were reproduced. Today, as in the past, owners feel a great sense of satisfaction in displaying their family arms as a proud heritage of their backgrounds.

Chapter Four

English Progenitors and Lineage

General

By the 14th century there were only a few Eldreds remaining in England and they were divided into two groups – one living in Sussex and the other in Lincolnshire.

Many Eldreds in America can trace their ancestry to a small hamlet located in the north-western part of Suffolk, England – very close to the Norfolk county line. This hamlet is called Knettishall (variations in spelling can be found, for example, Knattishall, Kettishall, Gnatshall and Gnatsell) and is regarded as the place where the Eldreds in America had their ancestral beginnings. The Eldreds in England have always shown a marked preference for the eastern and south-eastern counties.

English Progenitors

Four men became the progenitors of distinct Eldred families. They were John Eldred of Great Saxham and London; his nephew, Peter Eldred of London; Thomas Eldred of Ipswich, a distant relative of John and Peter; and William Eldred of Dover Castle, also a distant relative of the others.

John Eldred, known as 'the Traveller', was born in New Buckenham, Norfolk, England, in 1556, to which his father, John Eldred, had moved from Knettishall. As a young man, John moved to London. He was a prosperous businessman, becoming interested in foreign trade, and helping to organise a journey to Arabia. Records show that John Eldred and his associates

2. The deserted church of All Saints', Knettishall.

departed in February 1583 in a ship named *Tiger*. They arrived in Tripoli (north of Beirut, Lebanon) in May and travelled north to Aleppo, Syria and then to a place called Sir on the River Euphrates. They went down the river to Felleyah (Al Falliya) where they obtained 100 donkeys to carry their merchandise to Baghdad. They spent some time in this historic city, arranging for the shipment of their wares in boats on the River Tigris to Bassorah (Basra), where they stayed six months trading and bartering the goods they had brought with them. The merchandise which they obtained was primarily spices, especially nutmeg and cinnamon, which were in great demand in England. They were obviously skilful and successful traders, as they needed 70 barges to carry their goods back to England. In the diary kept by John Eldred, he said that each barge was towed by 14 men up the Tigris and that it took 44 days to reach Baghdad. There he joined a large caravan and his goods were transported by camels to Aleppo, arriving on 11 June 1584.

For the next three years Aleppo was John Eldred's headquarters, but he travelled extensively from there. He says in his diary:

> I made two journeys more into Baghdad and returned, by the way aforesaid, over the deserts of Arabia. And afterwards, being desirous of seeing other parts of the country, I did go from Aleppo to Antioch, which is 60 English miles, and from thence down to Tripoli again. There, I went aboard a small ship and came to Joppa (Jaffa). Thence I travelled to Rama, Lycia, Gaza, Jerusalem, Bethlehem, to the river Jordan and the Sea of Sodom [Dead Sea]. Then I returned to Joppa and by sea again to Tripoli ...

John and his companions embarked at Tripoli on 22 December 1587, for the return trip to England. They 'arrived safely in the River Thames, March 26, 1588, in the *Hercules* of London, with the richest shipload of merchants' goods ever known to come into the realm to this time'.

Most of the cargo belonged to John Eldred, and he became a very wealthy man. Soon after his return, he married Mary Revett of Risangles, Suffolk. Their first child, Emanuel, was born in 1590 but died in 1597. The second son, Revett, became the heir and eventually a baronet of the realm. There were eight other children, one of whom, Nathaniel, became the progenitor of the West Indies Eldreds. With plenty of capital for his business, John's wealth increased, as did his power and influence. He spent most of his time in London where he was an Alderman, also personal friend and trusted counsellor of Queen Elizabeth I and her successor, James I. He was on the Board of the directing Council of the Virginia Company under whose auspices Virginia and Massachusetts were settled. He was also a Royal Contractor, a commissioner for the Sale of Lands, a Farmer of Customs, and a holder of patents for the pre-emption of tin. His name appears many times on state papers and public records of that period.

John believed that Saxham Magna was the ancestral home of his Saxon forebears and so he purchased the estate, located in Suffolk, in 1597. On it he built a large mansion which he named Great Saxham Hall, but which his neighbours distastefully dubbed Nutmeg Hall. This estate remained in the family until 1745 when it was sold, there being no male Eldred heirs. Great Saxham Hall stood for almost 200 years before being destroyed by fire.

In 1632 John Eldred, the Traveller, died at the age of eighty. His estate exceeded $5,000,000, making him the richest Eldred of whom there is a record. On 8 December 1632, he was buried in the parish church at Great Saxham where his tomb is marked by a well-preserved brass about two feet long. In this is engraved his effigy in the robes of a London city alderman, the Eldred and Revett coat of arms, John's own coat armour as it was carried after his marriage to Mary Revett, and four commercial seals. There is a bust and monument to him erected in the same church by his son Revett with this inscription:

MEMORIAL SACRUM
John Eldred

New Buckingham in Norfolke was his first,
being in Babilon hee spent some parte
of his time; and the rest of his earthly
pilgrimage hee spent in London, and was
Alderman of that famous citeie.
His age LXXX

His Death
The Holy Land so called have I seene
And in the land of Babilon have bene.
But in the land when glorious saints doe live,
My soule doth crave of Christ a roome to give,
And there with Holy Angells Haliluiahs singe.
With joyfull voyce too God Our Heavenly King;
Not content but in thee, O Lord.

September 7, 1632

Peter, the son of John's older brother, also named Peter, went to London and became a member of the Grocers' Guild. Peter, known as 'the Grocer', secured a confirmation of his coat of arms *c*.1633 and 'the Eldreds of Broad Streete' were formally recognised. There is no record of any of his descendants emigrating to America, but many of them live in England today.

William Eldred, known as 'the Gunner' was born about 1565 and was of the Knettishall Eldreds. John refers to him as 'my kinsman' but the exact relationship is not known. William was probably a roving soldier of fortune. He was the Master Gunner of Dover Castle for several years. He wrote a book, published in 1634, entitled *The Gunner's Glasse* which gives an excellent description of big gun practice in those days. There is no evidence that his descendants emigrated to America.

Thomas Eldred of Ipswich, known as 'the Mariner' and 'the Merchant' was also of the Knettishall Eldreds. He was one of the crew who sailed with Thomas Cavendish around the world in 1586-88, a tremendous accomplishment at that time. His regular business as a ships' chandler earned him the 'Merchant' title. Thomas is of special interest to the descendants of Samuel Eldred of Massachusetts and Rhode Island, as he is probably their progenitor. Further information about Thomas and his family can be found in *English Lineage*.

English Lineage
John[1e] Eldred of Corby
One of the earliest Eldred documents is the will of John Eldred of Corby, Lincolnshire, which was written in Latin. It was dated 17 January 1489, and was proved 9 April 1489.

John's parentage is unknown and details concerning his life are limited to data extracted from his will. It seems likely that the elderly John was living with one of his children at the time of his death. They had moved from Corby to Knettishall, a distance of some 60 miles, which was a substantial trek in those days. The reason for the move is unknown.

John's will gives his age as 'well past the year of man by the roods of Books'. This means that he was more than 70, and would place his birth sometime before 1419. Four sons and two daughters are named in the will, but not a wife, whose name is unknown. She had probably died earlier.

The children are named thus:
1. *Nicholas[2], of whom below.
2. *Reginald[2], of whom below.
3. Martha[2], John of Corby's first daughter and 'third child'. Married Thomas Armstrong of Corby; NFK.
4. Robert[2], the will mentions son, Robert as 'fourth childe' and of Horncastle.
5. Ann[2], the will mentions daughter Ann Blackway as 'fifth childe'. NFK.
6. John[2] 'Sixth childe' and 'of Easthop'. He died after 1528. NFK.

Second Generation
Nicholas [2e] Eldred – born probably before 1454 in Corby. Married 1. Margaret ?; 2. Joan ?. Died *c.*1514, probably in Knattishall.

John Eldred's will (1489) mentions son Nicholas as 'first childe' and 'of Gnatsell'. Land records in Norfolk and Suffolk show that: 'In the fourth year of Henry VIII (1513), Geofry Walker confirms to Nicholas Eldred of Gnatsell, yeoman, a messuage and three crofts of land lying between the crofts of Walter Dyer and William Wykham'. Nicholas was a yeoman on rented land in Knettishall most of his life, but he was not to enjoy this particular 'messuage and crofts' for very long. County records contain this statement:

> In the fifth year of Henry VIII, William Warner pursuant to will of Nicholas Eldred, gentleman, of Corby and Knattishall, late deceased, confirms to William Eldred, oldest son of said Nicholas Eldred by his wife Margaret, and to his younger sons, Joseph and John by his wife, Joan, eight pieces of land lying between a croft of John Smelly's and the pieces of land called 'Bonders' to the use of the said William, Joseph, and John, in fee.

The last names of Nicholas' two wives, Margaret and Joan, are unknown; there were three sons mentioned in his will.

Children, by his wife Margaret: William[3], the great-grandfather of John Eldred (1556-1632) of London and Great Saxham. In 1592 John Eldred, 'the Traveller', submitted evidence to the Royal Herald substantiating his claim that Nicholas[2] Eldred used the Eldred coat of arms rightfully. The Herald acknowledged this claim when he confirmed John's use of the Eldred arms, and granted him his distinctive difference (Martlet) and crest (Arabian's head).

By his wife Joan: Joseph[3], mentioned in Nicholas' will; NFK.

John[3], mentioned in Nicholas' will; NFK.

Note. Nicholas[2e] is not in the direct lineage from John[1e] Eldred of Corby to Samuel[8e/1] Eldred; the direct lineage includes Reginald[2e], a brother of Nicholas[2e]. A brief sketch of Nicholas is included because of his son William's relationship to John Eldred of Great Saxham and confirmation of the Eldred coat of arms used by his great-great-grandfather, Nicholas[2e] Eldred. Reginald[2e] Eldred, probably born in Corby, married Agnes Coupe, daughter of Thomas Coupe, and died *c*.1528.

John Eldred's will (1489) mentions son Reginald as 'second childe' and 'of Gnatsell'. Like his brother, Nicholas, he was probably born in Corby and was a yeoman in Knettishall. The first written record for him is a lease in 1515: 'In the sixth year (1515) of Henry the VIII, Thomas Coupe of Garboldsham, confirmed to Reginald Eldred of Gnattsall, yeoman, and others, lands in Gnattsall lying between a messuage and a croft of John Eldred'. Reginald and Agnes had four sons and two daughters; they are mentioned in his will dated 4 February 1528. The names of these children show two traditions consistently followed by the Eldreds for many generations. The first is the strong preference for the name John (nearly every family had one or two) and, secondly, the practice of naming a son born late in the parents' lives the same as an older brother. To distinguish between them the first was called the Elder, the last, the Younger. The custom seems to have applied only to sons named John, but it occurred frequently.

Based upon Reginald's will, the name of his wife and children are known. Children:

1. John[3], the will states, 'my eldest childe', John the Elder. NFK.
2. *Thomas[3], of whom below.
3. Agnes[3].
4. Mary[3] (Eldred) Wynn.
5. Henry[5], the will mentions 'and the heirs of my deceased son, Henry'. NFK.
6. John[3], the will mentions 'my youngest childe, John the Younger'. NFK.

Third Generation

Thomas[3e] Eldred – born *c*.1460 in Knettishall. Married Agnes Lawsdall, a daughter of John Lawsdall, from Thurlby, Lincolnshire. Died after 1545 (determined from the will of his father-in-law).

Thomas Eldred is the only one of Reginald's family about whom we have further information. Born in Knattishall, he was a husbandman there. Like his father, he had four sons and two daughters; very little is known about them except for mention of them in the will of John Lawsdall (19 September 1545) which states 'Thomas Eldred of Knattishall, husband of my daughter Agnes; Nicholas Eldred, Symon Eldred,

3-5.   All Saints', Knettishall, 1981.

Robert Eldred and Thomas Eldred as my grandsons'. Both Thomas[3] Eldred and his wife are buried at Knettishall.
Children:
1. Symon[4].
2. Thomas[4], died in 1587 at Ipswich. NFK.
3. *Nicholas[4], of whom below.
4. Robert[4].
5. Ann[4].
6. Jane[4].

Fourth Generation

Nicholas[4e] Eldred – born 1496 in Knattishall. Married Bridget ? and died between August and October 1566. Buried at Knettishall.

Nicholas, the third son of Thomas Eldred, spent his life as a yeoman. His will, in Latin, dated 27 August 1566, was proved on 8 October of that year, indicating that he had died before the latter date. His wife, Bridget, is mentioned in the will as are four surviving children – there probably had been others.
Children:
1. William[5], living in Ipswich in 1566 when his father died. NFK.
2. Edmund[5], a tailor living in Ipswich in 1566. Died in London of the plague on 29 September 1569. NFK.
3. Alyce[5] (Allyce), married Stephen Rookwood (Rookewood). NFK.
4. *Thomas[5], the youngest child, of whom below.

Fifth Generation

Thomas[5e] Eldred, born c.1537, married Margery Studd, daughter of Richard Studd (Stud) of Ipswich, Suffolk, died before 1603 and is buried at St Clement's, Ipswich.

Thomas, the youngest son of Nicholas and Bridget, became one of the most renowned Eldreds. Like his brothers, he lived in Ipswich where he was known as the 'Mariner' and as the 'Merchant'. Actually he was a ship's chandler, that is, a merchandiser of seafaring supplies.

Nonetheless, when he was already 49 years old and had a successfully established business, he embarked on a long and dangerous voyage. He became a member of the crew of one of the ships in the expedition captained by Thomas Cavendish and destined to sail around the world. Only two other such voyages had ever been made. His decision to join the expedition is very surprising, considering not only his age and the fact that he was leaving his business, but also because he was leaving behind a wife and children. Chapter VI is devoted to a detailed account of that remarkable voyage.

Thomas owned, or perhaps built, a fine house in Brook Street, (Brookestreete), Ipswich. There were three notable paintings in this house that were later removed by John Eldred (1565-1646) of Colchester, Thomas' son, and placed in his country manor, Olivers, located near Stanway, Essex. One was a terrestrial globe with an inscription recording the date of Thomas' voyage around the world; the second was a four-masted ship, probably the one in which he made the voyage; the third was his portrait. These paintings were sold in later years and the Brook Street house became the *Neptune Inn* in the 1920s.

The birth or baptismal dates of Thomas and Margery's large family of 12 are recorded in the parish register of St Mary at Kay's, Ipswich. The parents died some-time before June 1603, for a document connected with their house in Brook Street, dated 21 June 1603, refers to 'Thomas Eldred, late of Ipswich, chandler, and his wife, Margery, deceased'.

Children:

1. Richard[6], baptised 8 January 1559. NFK.
2. Thomas[6], born 24 October 1561; baptised 8 November 1561, married Susan ? , died 1 May 1624 and is buried at St Clement's, Ipswich; will proved 23 June 1624 with many bequests.
3. Christine[6], baptised 11 May 1564, died 9 October 1646. NFK.
4. John[6], born 21 December 1565, married Elizabeth, daughter of John Rusham of London, moved to Colchester, Essex; a merchant, alderman, justice of the peace; owned Olivers in Essex. By grant of arms on 14 February 1630 he established the Eldreds of Essex. Died 9 October 1646 and was buried at Earls Colne, Essex. Had two sons, Edward and John, and two daughters, Mary and Aquill.
5. Mary[6], born 18 November 1566, married Henry Hamant. NFK.
6. Margery[6], baptised 8 July 1568, married Edmund Aldam (Aldman). NFK.
7. Jane[6], baptised 22 September 1569, married Richard Burlingame. NFK.
8. Susan[6], baptised 3 January 1571, married Samuel Greene. NFK.
9. Philip[6], baptised 8 August 1574; alderman and twice mayor of Hadleigh, head of the 'Eldreds of Hadleigh'. Died 22 February 1630.
10. *William[6], of whom below.
11. Ann(e)[6], baptised 18 September 1575. NFK.
12. Edward[6], baptised 28 March 1577. NFK.

Sixth Generation

William[6e] Eldred, baptised 2 December 1572 in Ipswich. Married but name of wife unknown. Died before 23 June 1624.

Almost no information exists about William. He is listed in his brother's will, dated in 1634, as being deceased. His one known child is listed also; perhaps William's brother, Thomas was godfather to the child.

Seventh Generation

Thomas[7], born c.1595, married Anna Watson, daughter of Samuel Watson, on 4 February 1617, died 1640; will dated 18 October 1640 and proved 4 December 1640.

Thomas was a sailor; Ipswich records in 1625 mention 'a Thomas Eldred in command of a ship lately come from Denmark', and he owned property in Barningham. His will of 1640 provided that his wife Anna will receive his house in Ipswich for her lifetime use, and thereafter will 'go to my eldest childe and namesake, Thomas Eldred, or his heirs if deceased'. The remainder of his estate in Ipswich was disposed according to his instructions, as follows:

> Give to my second childe, Charles Eldred, on his twentieth birthday, £75; to my third childe, Samuel Eldred on his twentieth birthday, £75; to my fourth childe, John Eldred, on his twentieth birthday, £25.

The remainder of my estate in Ipswich is to go to my fifth childe, Mary Eldred, on her eighteenth birthday, excepting that if it should amount to more than £25, that part more than £25 is to go to my son, Thomas Eldred.

To my son, John Eldred, my three crofts of land in Barningham.

To my third son, Samuel Eldred, the great sea-chest that my father, William Eldred of Bury had from his father, Thomas Eldred, the one who sailed around the world.

The children of Thomas[7e] and Anna Watson Eldred were all born in and recorded in Ipswich.

Children:

1. Thomas[8], born 20 December 1617, as recorded in the parish register, St Nicholas, Ipswich; NFK.

2. Charles[8], born 3 October 1619, as recorded at St Nicholas; the parish register at St Stephen's, Ipswich, shows: 'June 24 1639, married, Charles Eldred of Ipswich and Susan Bridges of Colchester'. Baptism of their daughter (at St Nicholas) is recorded on 1 May 1642.

3. *Samuel[8], of whom below.

4. John[8], under 20 years at date of father's will; NFK.

5. Mary[8], baptised 23 July 1626, NFK.

Eighth Generation

Samuel [8e/1] Eldred, born 27 November 1620, Ipswich. Married Elizabeth Miller, 25 November 1640 in Ipswich. She was the daughter of Daniel Miller, Needham Market. Died between 13 April 1697 and 12 February 1699 in North Kingstowne, Rhode Island.

Based upon strong circumstantial evidence it is widely believed that Samuel[8] Eldred, emigrated to the New World, dying in North America. Although at this time there is no solid proof, the probability is so strong that prominent genealogists who have researched and studied all known facts for many years have accepted this premise as an accurate one.

There are so many identical relationships in the records of an English Samuel[8] Eldred and an American Samuel[1] Eldred that it does not seem possible that they could be merely coincidental. Examples that support this conclusion are:

1. Persistent tradition among the descendants of Samuel, the immigrant, that the father of Samuel, or his ancestral forebear, was an Eldred named Thomas. Pride in descent from a prominent person, such as Thomas the Mariner with his circumnavigation of the globe, is natural, and the tradition of 'descent from a famous Eldred named Thomas' still persists today.

2. The *Genealogical and Personal Memoirs of Prominent Massachusetts Families* by Cutler and Adams (1910) includes a discussion on the several immigrant Eldreds: 'Information at hand states that Samuel Eldred was the son of one Thomas Eldred whose descendants also married into the Bollings of Virginia'.

3. Holden Eldred of the Lowell, Wisconsin, Eldreds, a descendant of Samuel[1] and a well-educated man, thoroughly versed in the history of his Eldred branch of the family tree, said in a letter to his brother, 'We are all descended from Samuel Eldred

who came to Rhode Island in 1660. He was the son of Thomas Eldred of Ipswich, England, and further back was descended from a famous Eldred who was a sailor on the first ship to sail round the world. I have heard my father tell the story as he heard it from his grandfather many many times'.

4. The wife of Samuel, the immigrant, was named Elizabeth, and they were married about 1640. These same facts apply to Samuel of Ipswich.

5. Samuel Eldred, the immigrant, made a deposition in court in Medford, Massachusetts in 1652, stating that he 'was about 32 years of age'. This places his birth in 1620, and Samuel of Ipswich was born in 1620.

6. The children of Samuel[1], the immigrant, were all born in America. The first child was named Elizabeth, the name of her mother, and the second child was named Samuel. The third child was named Mary; Samuel of Ipswich had an only sister named Mary, and their second daughter might have been named after her. The fourth child was named Thomas, the name of Samuel's father; the fifth child's name relationship cannot be established; but the sixth child was named John, and Samuel had a brother named John. The last child was named Daniel, and the father of Samuel's wife was Daniel. The selection of these names were in keeping with the custom of the times when the naming of children after their relatives was almost universal.

7. Samuel's father's will left him a considerable amount of money when he reached 20 years of age; he might very well have taken his legacy and young wife to America to seek greater opportunity.

   The conclusion that Samuel Eldred of Ipswich emigrated to America has not been arrived at haphazardly, and it seems logical in the absence of other evidence. The English lineage of Samuel Eldred, in condensed form, is given below as a summary of the previously known facts:

Samuel Eldred (1620-*c*.1697) **m**. Elizabeth Miller.
Thomas Eldred (*c*.1595-1640) **m**. Anna Watson.
William Eldred (bp.1572-*bef*.1624) **m**. unknown.
Thomas Eldred (*c*.1537-*bef*.1603) **m**. Margery Studd.
Nicholas Eldred (*c*.1496-1566) **m**. Bridget ?
Thomas Eldred (*c*.1460-1545) **m**. Agnes Lawsdall.
Reginald Eldred (*bef*.1439-*c*.1528) **m**. Agnes Coupe.
John Eldred of Corby (bef.1419-1489) **m**. unknown.

   Insofar as existing records speak truthfully, so far is this lineage faithfully stated.

Chapter Five

John Eldred of London and Great Saxham (1556-1632)

The original home of John Eldred's early ancestors was Corby, Lincolnshire. By the 16th and 17th centuries, Eldreds were in all of England's East Anglian counties. John, one of the family's most illustrious members, was born in 1556 and was baptised on 9 April of that year at New Buckenham, Norfolk. His father, another John and a husbandman, had moved there from Knettishall in Suffolk and died in 1558 when his son was only two years old.

In his will John Eldred (*c.*1518-58) left 'to the high altar there [New Buckingham] for tythes and oblations negligently forgotten and unpaid' twelve pence, and 'to the repairers of the highways of New Buckenham six shillings and eight pence'. He left his mother-in-law his 'house and tenements in Helmingham, otherwise called Morley, with the lands thereto belonging, both fee and copy' with the provision that after her death they should be divided between his two sons, Peter and John. His daughter, Margaret, received £10, half when she was 21 and the remainder the following year. His house and land in New Buckenham were left to his wife, Margaret, to be divided between his sons at her death. John asked in his will 'that my ii sons, John and Peter, be brought up to learning' and that 'the residue of all my goods, moveables and estates of what kind so ever they be' be given to his wife 'to bring up my children and to bring my body honestly to the grave ...'. He was buried in the churchyard of New Buckenham on 21 September 1558.

Whether John and Peter actually were 'brought up in learning' is unknown, as the period in their lives from 1558-83 is practically undocumented. They probably went to local schools as their names do not appear on the rolls of any of the major schools of the time or on any university list. John was apprenticed to a member of the Worshipful Company of Clothworkers in London and completed this period of servitude in 1588.

The details of John's apprenticeship are not clear, but it is certain that it was a fortunate one for him. His master was Edward Osborne, Lord Mayor of London in 1583. Trading with the Levant had lapsed for about twenty years, and Osborne was involved in getting it re-established. He and his partner, Richard Staper, began negotiations with the Grand Signior of Turkey in 1575 and, three years later, sent William Harborne to live in Constantinople as their agent. Through correspondence between Queen Elizabeth and the Grand Signior, English merchants acquired the right to trade in the Levant, and in 1581 Osborne and Staper promoted a highly successful voyage to Turkey. In September of that year, Queen Elizabeth gave them, with 'other such persons, Englishmen born, not exceeding the number of twelve', a monopoly in the vast Ottoman Empire (Turkey) trade for seven years. John Eldred was one of the 12 chosen by his master to trade under this monopoly. As it is very unlikely that he had any previous experience in foreign trade, he must have been selected for other qualities such as judgement and mathematical ability.

6. St Andrew's church, Great Saxham. John Eldred's two memorials, a bust on the wall and a brass on the chancel floor, are in this beautiful church.

7. Interior of St Andrew's church.

The voyage on which John travelled to the East was organised on a joint stock basis. Its purpose was to take William Barrett to Aleppo, Syria, to be the first English consul there, and to carry four adventurers on the first stage of their journey. They were John Newberry, who had travelled further east than any other Englishman, Ralph Fitch, James Story, a painter, and William Leedes, a jeweller. The four had letters from Queen Elizabeth to the King of Cambaia (India) and to the Emperor of China.

John's mission, and that of three others, was to trade in the Levant. The name of the ship was the *Tiger* and may well have been the inspiration for the First Witch's words in *Macbeth*: 'Her husband's to Aleppo gone, master o' th' Tiger'. The merchants took kerseys (or carsies – coarse woollen cloths), cloths, tin and various pieces of haberdashery valued at £2,000, of which John seems to have contributed £380-worth. They also had an unspecified amount of money in ducats. In Aleppo they bought coral, amber, soap, broken glass and other small trifles.

John's account of this voyage, in which he tried to recreate for his readers the sights he saw, was published in Hakluyt's *The Principal Navigations ... of the English Nation*. He wrote that the *Tiger* left Falmouth on 11 March 1583 after some delay and went through a severe storm before it reached Tripoli, north of Beirut in the Lebanon, on 1 May. In Tripoli, which John described as being 'about the bigness of Bristol', the merchants stayed at the 'Fondeghi Ingles' or house of the English. A most interesting sight was 'a bank of moving sand ... according to an old prophecy ... like to swallow up and overwhelm the town'. He also noted 'mulberry trees on which there grow abundance of silk worms, wherewith they make great quantity of very white silk'. They left Tripoli on 14 May and crossed the mountain range of Libanus. On 17 May they were in Hammah (Syria), which had 'fallen and falleth more and more to decay ... because it cost many men's lives to win it, the Turk will not have it repaired; and hath written in the Arabian tongue over the castle gate ... cursed be the father and the son that shall lay their hands to the repairing hereof'.

They arrived in Aleppo on 21 May. John reported that it was 'the greatest place of traffic for a dry town that is in all these parts; for hither resort Jews, Tartarians, Persians, Armenians, Egyptians, Indians and many sorts of Christians, and enjoy freedom of their consciences and bring thither many kinds of rich merchandises'. William Barrett stayed in Aleppo, as consul, and the others left by camel on 31 May for Birrah (called Sir), a town at the head of the Euphrates river. They bought food in Birrah and prepared a small flat-bottomed boat to carry them to Felugia, a journey of 28 days. They stopped at night, cooked their rice or bruised wheat over a camp fire and then the merchants slept on the boat and the sailors on the shore.

During the trip they bartered with Arabians, 'glasses, combs, coral ... amber' for 'milk, butter, eggs and lambs'. John described the people as being 'like those vagabond Egyptians which heretofore have gone about in England ... their women all without exception wear a great round ring in one of their nostrils, of gold, silver, or iron ...'. He admired their swimming skills, as they brought pails of milk out to the ship on their heads, but bewailed their thievery, saying 'they stole a casket of mine from under my man's head as he was asleep'.

On 28 June they were in Felugia where they stayed seven days trying to get camels to carry them on the Babylon. There were none available, so they settled for 100 donkeys instead and crossed the desert at night to avoid the scorching heat. They passed the old city of Babylon, including the Tower of Babel, an edifice made of huge bricks 'almost as high as the stone work of St Paul's steeple in London'. To get to New Babylon they had to cross a 'great bridge made with boats chained together with two mighty chains of iron'. The merchandise was brought to the city on rafts floated on inflated goats' skins which were then deflated, carried back and used again.

Although New Babylon was 'a place of very great traffic and a very great thorough-fare from the East Indies to Aleppo', there was little demand there for the goods brought in by John and his fellow merchants. He reported:

> Whereas we had thought to have sold in this place great store of our commodities, we cannot sell ... This town is so full of carsies and tin, most bought at Aleppo of William Barrett, which were the tin and cloth that came in the *Emmanuel*. Tin here is as good cheap as it is in Aleppo, and cloth also, God send it to mend or otherwise this voyage of ours will make no profit.

Two of the merchants stayed in New Babylon (Iraq) with £1,000-worth of merchandise, while the others, taking £764-worth with them, set out on a 28-day journey to Basra, Iraq, a city just below the merging point of the Tigris and the Euphrates. There the stock was again divided, four of the merchants taking £400-worth on to the East Indies, while John and William Shales began a six-month residence in Basra to sell the remainder. Here, too, they had difficulty. John wrote, 'we have not sold, neither can we sell all of our commodities ... our carsies here are not worn ... we have offered our commodities at a price very reasonable ... but no man would deal with us'. They finally gave up the project and were ready to sail for Persia when two Venetian merchants arrived from Ormus (Iran). These merchants had located spices worth 10,000 ducats but did not have enough money to purchase them. John and Shales, however, had available funds and bargained with the Venetians very profitably for some of the spices and so stayed on in Basra. Two months later, a Frenchman arrived who bought some of their goods partially on credit at 15 per cent interest.

By this time, pirates who attacked merchant ships were making travel outside Basra unsafe. John wrote that no ship had dared leave the port for more than four months, so he had arranged for all of his goods to be shipped by camel caravan. He had:

> four somes of large cinnamon, fourteen somes and a half of middle cinnamon, three somes and a half of nutmegs, one some and a half of ginger, one some and a third part of cloves, four some and a half fusses of cloves, 197 turbands fine, and one chest of gilded pusillanes ... all these goods have been in readiness this month wishing every day our departure, which God grant may be shortly, for here we spend and our money eateth, and that which is worse, we fear we shall lose our passage from Baget to Aleppo, except we depart very shortly.

They finally loaded this merchandise onto 70 boats, rather than camels, and joining other merchants began a 44-day trip up the river to Babylon. There they paid

8. *(above)* Coat of arms and crest used by John Eldred (1556-1632). Arms confirmed and crest granted in 1592 by Garter King of Arms.

9. *(above right)* Eldred-Revett family coat of arms.

10. *(right)* Revett family coat of arms.

customs, bought camels, hired men to drive them and obtained permission for the next stage of their journey. They had a large caravan of camels and *en route* across the desert had to pay a duty of 40 shillings on each to ensure safe passage. They arrived in Aleppo on 11 June 1584, having been away from home for more than a year, and they were to be away for another four.

John made at least two more trips back to Babylon, spending about two years there in all. Two of his colleagues had established themselves in Cairo where they needed money for trade as the Egyptians had little desire for English commodities. John planned to take them 4,000 ducats in 1586, but just before his departure the English consul in Aleppo died and the Turkey Company ordered John to take his place. His responsibilities included supervising the English merchants in the area and running a hostelry for them. Among his other duties he had to imprison Englishmen trying to trade without Company membership, and ensure a correct standard of weights and measures. He dealt with Turks, Venetians and Frenchmen. The Company paid its consuls very low salaries, if any, but John probably collected a consulage fee of about 2 per cent on all Company goods passing through the city.

John went to the Holy Land in 1587, visiting Jaffa, Jerusalem, Bethlehem, and the Red Sea, and at some time during his years in the mid-east he reached Egypt.

Hostility between England and Spain was increasing at this time, making the seas around both countries unsafe for travel, but on 22 December 1587 John embarked on the *Hercules* for home. Foul weather and enemy attacks made it an extremely difficult and hazardous trip lasting three months, but cargo (see *Appendix I*) worth £37,683 was landed in England on 26 March 1588, not long before the Spanish Armada sailed up the Channel. John's share of the profit appears to have been about £10,000.

Thus John became a well-to-do merchant and he soon set about acquiring an appropriate social status. He married Mary Revett, daughter of a Suffolk landowner, and bought a house in Basinghall Street, London, described as the third largest of the 'divers fair houses for merchants at Blackwell Hall', the famous cloth market was located nearby. When Richard Whittington was Mayor of London, there was a regulation that 'no foreigner or stranger should sell any woollen cloth but in the Blackwell Hall, upon pain of forfeiture thereof'. It seems likely that John was involved in the cloth trade throughout his life. As an interesting detail, he had a black servant who died and was buried in London. 'Blackamoors' were something of a rarity in London in the early 17th century.

John and Mary's first child, Emanuel, was born in 1590 but soon died. The next year another son, Revett, was born and was to become John's chief heir. There was another son, then three daughters and finally three more sons and a daughter. Mary died when the last daughter (who survived) was born in 1613. She was buried in the church of St Michael, close to their London house in Basinghall Street, as were some of her children, including Sir Revett Eldred and his wife Anne. There is no record of their exact resting place. The church itself, built after the Great Fire of 1666, was demolished about eighty years ago, and its site is marked by a plaque.

In 1597 John bought a country estate in Great Saxham near Bury St Edmunds in Suffolk for about £3,000, later adding park land to it for which he paid £800. It is

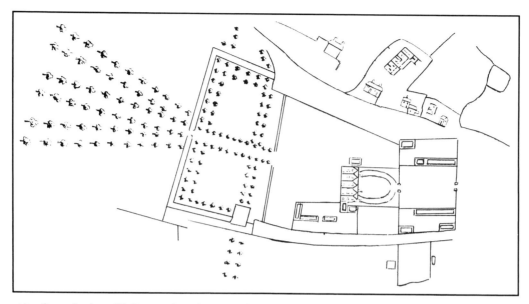

11.   Great Saxham Hall, sometimes known as Nutmeg Hall as John Eldred introduced nutmegs into England. This sketch is taken from a survey made for John Eldred in 1729.

traditionally suggested that he chose Great Saxham because he considered himself to be descended from the Anglo-Saxon King Eadred, who had a palace there. This is possible, as he was seeking social status at the time, but the availability of the site was probably a more potent factor in his choice. The Manor of Great Saxham had five gables with a large central porch and was known as Nutmeg Hall by local citizens because John had introduced nutmegs into England. The original house burned down in 1779, and the present Great Saxham Hall was built near the old site. The only visible remains of John's occupancy of Great Saxham Hall are a few oak trees from the long avenues that he planted in the park.

Although he had a large home and estate, John did little to establish himself in country society as he spent most of his time in London. The estate was presumably managed by a bailiff and the profit from it, in addition to the trade John was conducting himself in London, contributed to the sizeable fortune he was able to accumulate. In the country he was overshadowed by his neighbours, who on occasion entertained the king. John was never so honoured, but in 1611 he did receive a New Year's gift of £650 from James I.

The Eldred family had borne arms in the Middle Ages, and John probably used his ancestral armorial bearings before confirmation by the College of Arms in 1592. The arms confirmed were the same as those used by Nicholas Eldred (c.1454-1513), his great-great-grandfather, and his ancestors. The crest was new – a Turk's head as a memento of his travels, evidence that trade as a source of wealth did not embarrass him. John also probably became something of a celebrity when Hakluyt's

South Front

12. Great Saxham Hall in 1774, before the fire. The house was owned by Hutchinson Mure from 1745-94.

13. Saxham Hall in 1981, owned by Lady M. Stirling.

Principal Navigations was published. In 1604 he received a year's appointment as Master of the Clothworkers' Company and at the same time was made an alderman for the ward of Faringdon Without. The latter appointment lasted only three months and he was fined £500 for resigning before his term expired.

John retained his interest in trade with the middle-east and by 1600 was treasurer of the newly founded Levant Company, a position of great responsibility. Nevertheless, he became involved in a variety of other trading enterprises, the most important being the East India Company. The Dutch trade with the East Indies was threatening the Levant Company's market in spices, so John and some colleagues decided to mount their own enterprise to the Indies in a joint stock venture. Queen Elizabeth gave them a 45-year monopoly, and on 31 December 1600 the East India Company charter was signed by 218 members, with John as one of the directors. The first voyage in 1601 was very successful as were two later ones. The profits from these more than covered the loss on the fourth voyage when two ships were wrecked.

The detailed records of the East India Company include an account of John's activities as one of its directors. For example, he was among those chosen to inspect the ships for the first voyage. They selected five ships carrying a total crew of 500 men. The directors had to hire the crew, buy food for them and also acquire the commodities to be traded. John Eldred and Richard Staper were nominated 'to provide all the cloths and kerseys to be sent on the voyage'. In November 1600, John recommended his relative, Thomas Eldred, to be captain or master of a ship. After interviewing him, the directors agreed to give him a post. King James I was interested in the voyage. He directed John to write to all the Company's servants, requesting the 'reserving of all strange fowls and beasts etc. for the King and Council'.

Little is known of John's association with the Russia or Muscovy Company, as many of its records were destroyed by fire in the 19th century. There was a demand for English cloth in Russia and he probably supplied it for the Company voyages. However, competition curtailed profits and it is unlikely that he made much from this investment.

John was involved in the Virginia Company throughout its existence from 1606-24. James I appointed 14 men, of whom John was one, to form the King's Council of Virginia and to be responsible for the government of the English settlers in North America. Their instructions were to

> have full power and authority ... in our name, to give directions to the councils of the several colonies ... for the good government of the people planted in these parts and for the good ordering and disposing of all causes happening within the same, the same to be done for the sustenance thereof, as near to the common laws of England.

Membership of the Council entailed heavy governmental responsibility and was a great privilege. It was soon realised that the colony would not yield large supplies of precious metals nor provide a quick overland route to Cathay. Because the Company ran into debt, John's considerable investments had not been profitable, but his membership had been an honour.

14. **Brass memorial in St Andrew's church, Great Saxham, with an effigy of John Eldred and his family and business coats of arms.** The Latin inscription translates thus:

Accomplished my life's course trading abroad
Visiting Egypt, Arabia and Syria
[My] wreaths of distinction and merit have ceased to be woven [made]
[My] son's [only] riches are [my] everlasting name
I die fortunate and full of years [:] even the longest
Course of life comes to an end in the tomb.

" Curriculum vitæ peregrè mercando peregi,
Ægyptum, atque Arabas, Syrosque visens :
Eximiæ reduci et meritæ cessere coronæ
Nati, divitiæ, perenne nomen.
Fœlix, grandævus morior : longissima quamvis
Sit vitæ viâ—terminus sepulchrum.

Might all my travells me excuse
For being deade and lying here ;
Or if my Riches well to use
For life to death might mee endeare ;
I had my fate or quite outgone,
Or purchase't death's compassion
But riches can no ransome buy
Nor travells passe the destiny.

Revettus Eldred Ar : Filius et heres mæstissimus
Defuncti hoc monumentum posuit Septembris 7º, Aº Domini 1632."

In 1611, both John and Thomas Eldred were on a list of merchants trading with France. John was also a member of the Hudson Company of 1610 and its successor, the Company for the Discovery of the North-west Passage, whose president was Henry, Prince of Wales. He traded with the Netherlands, attempted to get into the Brazilian trade and dabbled in privateering in the West Indies. The author-historian K. R. Andrews described him as 'not simply a rich and powerful merchant, but a moving spirit in the pioneer enterprise of his day'.

Customs duties were a source of friction between the merchants and the Crown, and John did not escape this problem. For some time the Levant Company had collected an imposition on every hundred-weight of currants imported by merchants who were not members of the Company. They offered to pay this directly to the queen if she would grant them a monopoly on the Levant trade. Faced with the loss of their charter, John and his colleagues agreed to pay the queen £4,000 a year for its retention and the privilege of collecting the imposition. In 1603, probably in an attempt to make a more advantageous arrangement with the new king, James I, they declared that they could no longer afford to pay the £4,000. He responded by 'farming' the imposition on currants out to the Earl of Suffolk for £5,500 a year, and the Levant Company had to pay this amount to have their charter renewed. John was personally involved in a long-drawn-out case on these customs for he had refused to pay £157 on 30 butts of currants brought in on his ships. The king settled the matter against the customs farmers and in John's favour. He was not so lucky in trying to avoid paying customs on tobacco brought in from the West Indies. However, by the time the court declared against him, the case had been in process for so long that he had sold the tobacco, made his money and actually lost very little in the transaction.

King James I was always in need of funds and, in 1609, he arranged to sell Crown lands to eight syndicates, one of which was headed by John Eldred. This position could have been a stepping stone to a government office, but John apparently preferred to remain in trade. It was a profitable assignment – in December 1609 John Eldred and William Whitmore, for the syndicate, loaned the king £30,000 at 10 per cent interest. At the end of the year the king was not only unable to repay the principal and interest, but also needed an additional £17,000. Under new contract, he gave the syndicate £50,000 in lands which were scattered all over England; in disposing of them John became a real estate agent. Among the acquisitions he had a half share in the ownership of the priory in New Buckenham for which the rent was £16 a year. This amount was given to the vicar of New Buckenham to be used for charity. John also contributed to a charity in his ward in London.

In 1621 John was summoned before a committee of the House of Commons concerning conditions at the Fleet Prison which he owned jointly with Sir Henry Lello. Their warden was accused of over-charging for beds in rooms shared by 10 men, depriving the prisoners of food, and stealing from them. John testified in the Committee's investigation of these abuses and an impeachment was drawn up against the warden.

John's extensive business transactions involved him in a number of court cases, the most serious of which seems to have been with his son-in-law, Sir Samuel Tryon. John and his son, Revett, loaned Samuel £5,000 in 1622 which they themselves had been forced to borrow as, at the time, they didn't have the cash on hand. As security they took a mortgage on Sir Samuel's estates for 80 years. This deal caused considerable trouble and had little promise of profit, but was undertaken in the spirit of providing friendly assistance. Two years later later Samuel had paid neither the principal nor the 10 per cent interest, so John attempted to make a direct collection of the rents on the Tryon estate. Samuel instructed his tenants to pay no rent and undertook to 'weary out' the Eldreds 'with many suits'. Thus John was 'like to lose both land and money and stood at great loss ... paying interest and receiving none'. Furthermore, it was found that the estate was worth only £400 a year, not even enough to cover the interest. To obtain redress against the 'unkind carriage of Sir Samuel Tryon', John took the case to Chancery, and in 1630 when he made his will it was just dragging to a close. Sir Samuel had died, but his son continued the struggle.

Revett and his father seem to have been partners during the 1620s. Revett joined the Levant Company but that was the limit of his entry into trade. They seem to have shared the Basinghall Street house and to have had a close relationship. Revett's inheritance included 'the manor of Great Saxham and all and every my manors, messuages, lands, meadows, pastures, liberties, tenements, and hereditaments whatsoever as well as freehold and copyhold situate, lying, being and standing within the counties of Suffolk, Norfolk and Lincoln and elsewhere in this realm of England'. He had purchased his partner's half interest in the office of 'Warden of the Fleet and custody of the prison and gaol of the Fleet' but specified in his will that the office be returned to Lello's executors for £8,000 and the money be given to Revett.

There were other grants in the will. To the 'honest and neediest poor people' of Great Saxham, £10; to Revett's wife, 'as a token of my love and good will to her', £20 and his 'damask linen-cloth lately bought of Sir William Curteous'; and to his two servants, £5 each.

John, obviously aware that ignoring his other relatives in his will would anger them, stated in it:

> I do earnestly request my two sons-in-law and the said John Eldred the younger to accomplish my desire and said intent ... as in right and conscience they ought to do, they being only trusted by me with the said lease and monies, every one of them having formerly tested my love and kindness towards them in other things ...

At about this time John ordered his tomb, almost certainly from the London sculptor, Maximilian Colt, who had made Queen Elizabeth's in Westminster Abbey. He chose to have a small bust of himself, dressed in his alderman's robes, a portrait from life that even shows the warts on his face. The tomb was probably not set up until after his death, as in his will he requested that he be buried in London beside his wife, should he die in Basinghall Street, or at Great Saxham if he died in Suffolk. He died in 1632 and was buried on 8 December before the altar of the Great Saxham Church, 'without funeral pomp but in a comely Christian and decent manner'. His bust was set up overlooking the chancel. His relatives did not know his actual age, but guessed it to be about eighty and had that engraved on the inscription. Revett had a memorial brass placed to mark the grave, showing John in his alderman's robes and

15. Signature of John Eldred from a page in the Warden's Account Book of the Clothworkers' Company, London, England.

16. (*above*) Coloured bust of John Eldred in St Andrew's church, Great Saxham, and (*right*) a detail of the inscription beneath.

Memoriæ Sacrum
Iohn Eldred

NEW BVCKINGAM IN NORFOLKE WAS HIS FIRST
BEING, IN BABILON HEE SPENT SOME PARTE
OF HIS TIME, AND THE REST OF HIS EARTHLY
PILGRIMAGE HEE SPENT IN LONDON, AND WAS
ALDERMAN OF THAT FAMOVS CITTIE.
HIS AGE LXXX
HIS DEATH
THE HOLY LAND SO CALLED I HAVE SEENE
AND IN THE LAND OF BABILON HAVE BENE
BVT IN Y LAND WHERE GLORIOVS SAINTS DOE LIVE
MY SOVLE DOTH CRAVE OF CHRIST A ROOME TO GIVE
AND THEIRE WITH HOLY ANGELLS HALILVIAHS SINGE
WITH IOYFVLL VOYCE TOO GOD OVR HEAVENLY KING
NO CONTENT BVT IN THE O LORD.

17.   Eldred's thorn, a favourite seat of John Eldred, is located in a field about half a mile north of Saxham Hall.

listing his major exploits and interests – the City of London, the Clothworkers' Company, the Levant, East India and Russia Companies, and the shields of both of his parents.

Revett did not follow in his father's footsteps in trade, preferring to be a country gentleman. Tradition has it that he often sat under a favourite thorn tree in the park, which is now called 'Eldred's thorn'. Charles I made him a baronet in 1641. He died in 1652 and was buried in London beside his mother.

Upon the death of Anne, Revett's widow, the estate passed to Revett's great-nephew, John, who married Elizabeth Hervey. The Manor of Great Saxham was sold in 1745 to Hutchinson Mure. The memory of John Eldred 'The Traveller' has been preserved in the history of England, in local tradition, in the writings of his prominent contemporaries such as Sanderson, Hakluyt and Purchas, and in the records of the different enterprises in which he participated and through which he created his wealth. Some of his descendants emigrated to America in the late 18th to early 19th centuries and settled in Pennsylvania.

Note: *The original thesis on John Eldred of London and Great Saxham was prepared by Clare Gittings of Hertford, Herts., England. It has served as the principal basis for the condensed version that appears above.*

Born in Sussex, England, in 1954, her parents are the writers Jo Manton and the late Robert Gittings. In 1975 she earned a degree in history from the University of East Anglia, Norwich, where her dissertation was a biographical work on John Eldred. While at college she published a book, Brasses and Brass Rubbing, *now a standard work on the subject. From 1975-9 she researched and wrote a Master of Literature thesis at Oxford University on funeral rituals and attitudes toward death in early modern England. This was published in 1984 under the title* Death, Burial and the Individual in Early Modern England *and appeared in paperback in 1989.*

Clare Gittings spent eight years teaching in primary schools near Hertford. From 1986-8 she was a volunteer with Voluntary Service Overseas training primary school teachers in the Republic of Maldives. She now holds the position of Education Officer at the National Portrait Gallery, London.

The condensation of Clare Gittings' thesis for this book was prepared by Luella Eldridge of Silver Spring, Maryland. Before her retirement she was employed by the U.S. Department of State in its foreign service and in Washington, D.C. She has a Master of Arts degree from George Washington University in Washington, D.C. and is now engaged in various genealogical projects.

Brass from Great Saxham.

Chapter Six

Thomas Eldred The Mariner:
Around the World in Seven Hundred and Eighty Days

Thomas Eldred (*c.*1537-*c.*1603), a merchant 'of good report' and tallow-chandler of Ipswich, England, was the great-grandfather of Samuel Eldred who came to Massachusetts in 1641. He was a noted mariner whose greatest adventure was a trip around the world with Captain Thomas Cavendish (Candish) beginning in 1586 and ending in 1588.

Documentation has not yet been found concerning Thomas' parents nor the dates and places of their birth and death but there is evidence that he was the husband of Margery, daughter of Richard Studd (Stud) of Ipswich who was also a tallow-chandler. Among his 12 known children were John Eldred, Alderman of Colchester, who purchased the estate of Olivers in Stanway, Essex, and Philip Eldred, twice Mayor of Hadleigh, Suffolk. Thomas was probably a distant cousin of John Eldred (1556-1632), the prominent merchant-traveller-adventurer of London and Great Saxham. They were at least acquainted, as records show that John sponsored Thomas for an officer position on a voyage with the East India Company on 7 November 1600.

Thomas and Margery (Studd) Eldred lived in the parish of St Mary-at-Quay's Ipswich, from 1558-77. The parish register of baptisms includes entries for Richard (8 Jan. 1559), Thomas (8 Nov. 1561), Christine (11 May 1564), William (2 Dec. 1572), Philip (8 Aug. 1574) and Edward (28 Mar. 1577). Their other children are not recorded in this register but data on tombstones and in wills reveal John (b. 21 Dec. 1565), Mary (bapt. 18 Nov. 1566), Margery (bapt. 8 July 1588), Jane (bapt. 22 Sept. 1569), Susan (bapt. 3 Jan. 1571) and Ann (bapt. 18 Sept. 1575).

The will of Ralph Goodwin, dated 1562, shows that the Eldred family was living in his house in Brooke Street, an area of Ipswich described as pleasant and prestigious. The Eldreds were still there when Ralph Goodwin's widow, Elizabeth, died in 1576. The will stipulated that the property be sold after her death, so the Eldreds probably had to move at that time.

Whatever doubts surround the parentage and dates of birth and death of Thomas Eldred, historians agree that he was one of the '123 persons of all sorts' to sail with Thomas Cavendish on his round-the-world voyage in 1586-88. His participation in this adventure is confirmed by inscriptions on contemporary paintings of Thomas Eldred, as well as by references in the Court Records of the East India Company and in the preamble to the grant of arms made to his son, John Eldred, merchant, of Colchester, some years later.

The background to the voyage is an interesting one. The young nobleman and courtier Thomas Cavendish of Trimley St Martin, near Felixstowe in Suffolk, had dissipated his inheritance in extravagant living. A man of his time, both gallant and enterprising, he hoped to retrieve his lost fortune by mounting a private expedition

18. Portrait of Thomas Eldred from a group of three panel paintings originally located in Olivers, Stanway, Essex, the home of Thomas' son John.

against Spain, in particular against their ships and settlements on the coast of South America. He was encouraged by the successes of Hawkins and Drake and, now that war with Spain had been declared, depredations on the Spaniards were regarded as both lawful and heroic.

He fitted out, at his own expense, a squadron of three vessels: the *Desire* (120 tons), the *Content* (60 tons) and the *Hugh Gallant* (a bark of 40 tons), and manned them with a mixed crew of men from various parts of England – men who shared with him a common taste for adventure, courage and, no doubt, cupidity. At that time seafaring was a hazardous business. Ships were tiny by modern standards, vast areas of the globe remained unknown and uncharted, and the chances of returning from such a voyage were less than fifty-fifty. Why a man of mature years like Thomas Eldred, married with a family and business, was ready to stake all in this manner is puzzling, though the rewards were such as to tempt the least adventurous of men – and to judge by his kinsman, John Eldred of Great Saxham and his journey to the Middle East, the Eldreds of that time were not lacking in enterprise.

Be that as it may, the little fleet under the command of its self-appointed admiral, Thomas Cavendish, in the *Desire*, set sail from Plymouth on 21 July 1586, nearly nine years after Drake began his epic voyage around the world. The ships were well supplied with arms, ammunition and provisions. On board the *Hugh Gallant* was Master Francis Pretty, another Suffolk man, whose account of the voyage was published by Richard Hakluyt in his *Principal Voyages and Discoveries of the English Nation*. All quotations which appear in this article are from that work.

Holding to a sou'westerly course, the squadron crossed the Bay of Biscay and, leaving the Canary Islands on the starboard side, followed the west coast of Africa down past Rio del Ora as far as Sierra Leone. Here they put in after being at sea for just over a month. A raiding party went ashore and attacked the township near the mooring site, which consisted of about a hundred houses 'with their yards paled in

19. View of Thomas Eldred's house on Fore Street, in the parish of St Clement's, Ipswich.

and kept very clean, as well in their streets as in their houses'. The raiders took what little spoil there was, set light to a few houses and returned to their ships.

Three days later, the natives avenged themselves on the pirates. A party of English sailors went ashore to wash their shirts. As they were so engaged, inhabitants armed with bows and arrows fell upon them so suddenly that many were hurt, retreating to their boats. Amongst the wounded was William Pickman, a soldier, shot in the thigh. He tried to pluck the arrow out of his leg, but the shaft snapped off, leaving the arrow head buried in his flesh. Rather than face the primitive surgery of those days, Pickman lied and told the surgeon that he had plucked out all the arrow. 'Where-upon', we are told, 'the poison wrought so that night, that he was marvellously swollen, and all his belly and privie parts were as black as ink, and the next morning he died'.

The day before they left Sierra Leone, they watered their ships and replenished their larder with locally-caught fish and fruit such as lemons and plantains, a kind of banana. A few days later, blessed with a favourable wind, they set sail for the coast of South America. It must have been a long, tedious voyage as it lasted throughout the rest of September and all of October, and meant passing through the Doldrums, that area of the ocean near the equator where few winds blow. Even so, Cavendish made better time than Drake had done over the same stretch of water. His first sight of land, on 31 October, was of 'a great mountain with a high round nob on the top', no doubt the famous landmark seen by all who arrive at Rio de Janeiro by sea.

Over seven weeks had passed since Cavendish and his men had stood on dry land. The ships needed to be trimmed and the pinnace, stored in the hold of the *Desire*, assembled. Even more important was the need to replenish their supplies of food and water, so the Admiral dropped anchor off the island of San Sebastian, and every-one set about preparing for the next stage of their voyage. After three weeks ashore, all was ready and they resumed their journey southwards.

By 16 December they had reached a point some three-quarters of the way down the coast of modern Argentina, and the following day Cavendish led them into a good harbour which he named after his ship, Port Desire, the name by which it is known to this day. Their search for food was rewarded with the discovery of large colonies of seals and penguins. Francis Pretty describes the seals as being of

> a wonderful great bigness, huge and monstrous of shape and, for the forepart of their bodies, cannot be compared to anything better than to a lion. Their head and neck are full of rough hair; their feet are in manner of a fin, and in form like a man's hand. Their young are marvellous good meat and being boiled or roasted are hardly to be known from lamb or mutton ... Also, the fowls that were there were very good meat and great store of them. They have burrows in the ground like conies, for they cannot fly. They fish and feed in the sea for their living, and breed on shore.

The harbour looked to be an ideal place for graving and cleaning the bottoms of the ships, and this work kept the men busy until after Christmas. During their stay in Port Desire two of them were wounded by a party of Indians in much the same circumstances as those in which William Pickman died in Sierra Leone. As on that occasion, the English were ambushed whilst washing their linen at a well. The Indians, notes Pretty, 'were as wild as a buck, or any other wild beast'. They painted their bodies with a red dye and one man whom the English managed to catch had feet 18 ins. long. The same red dye was used to paint the long stones with which they covered their graves on the cliff tops. When a tribesman died, he was buried along with his bow and arrows and his personal ornaments made of fine sea shells.

Cavendish weighed anchor on 28 December and continued to run along the coast of South America as far south as the entrance to the dreaded Straits of Magellan, which they reached on 6 January 1587. Some 300 miles long, at places very narrow, the Straits provided a passage for ships proceeding from the Atlantic to the Pacific oceans. It is one of the most inaccessible and lonely places in the world, and passes through a bleak, inhospitable landscape of sea and islands, craggy rocks and 'monstrous high hills and mountains'. Even today it is seldom used. It must have been an awesome and terrifying challenge to the men who sailed in those small ships which Cavendish commanded.

They had not proceeded far through the Straits when they picked up from the shore a Spaniard who told them that he was one of a party of 23, two of whom were women, who were the sole survivors of 400 Spaniards who had been left there three years previously. They had been given the task of fortifying the Straits, 'to the end that no other nation should have passage through into the South Sea saving their own'. They had built a town, called King Philip's City, which the English ships came upon two days later and found to be deserted. Pretty describes it as well-fortified and well-sited for wood and water, and it had its own churches:

> They had laws very severe amongst themselves, for they had erected a gibbet whereupon they had done execution upon some of their company. It seemed that their whole living for a great space was altogether upon mussels and limpets. There was nothing else to be had except some deer which came out of the mountains down to the fresh rivers to drink. During the time that they were there, which was two years at the least, they could never have anything to grow, or in any wise prosper. The Indians oftentimes preyed upon them, until their victuals grew so short, (their store being spent which they had brought with them out of Spain), and having no means to renew them that they died like dogs in their houses, and in their clothes, wherein we still found them at our coming, until that in the end the town was wonderfully tainted with the smell and savour of dead people. The rest which remained alive were driven to forsake the town and go along the sea-side, and seek their victuals to preserve them from starving. They so lived for the space of a year or more with roots, leaves and sometimes a fowl which they might kill with their piece ...

The sorry sight of these citizens of King Philip's ill-fated city in the Magellan Straits matched that of some of the early English settlers at Jamestown, Virginia, soon afterwards, and graphically illustrates the hardships and privations suffered by the first European colonists in the Americas. We do not know what became of that party of Spaniards who, it seems, were hoping to reach the River Plate, nor what succour, if any, they received from Cavendish and his men. Pretty closes his account of the incident by saying, with a suggestion of reverence for its unfortunate inhabitants, 'in this place we watered and wooded well and quietly. Our general named the town Port Famine'.

It was now 14 January and Cavendish resumed his slow and tortuous passage through the Straits, watching out for hidden banks and shoals and for lone pinnacle rocks which sprung up from the bed of the channel. Violent tides and squalls were other hazards to be faced. From time to time they came upon a congenial bay where they dropped anchor. It was one such spot which Cavendish, out of respect for his sovereign, named 'Elizabeth Bay'. One of his company named Grey, a carpenter aboard the *Hugh Gallant*, died there and was buried in the bay.

A couple of leagues further on, they discovered the mouth of a fresh water river which Cavendish explored in a small boat for a distance of some three miles. They encountered a party of man-eating Indians whom they identified as being the same people who had attacked and preyed upon the Spanish settlers at King Philip's City, from whom they had stolen knives and rapiers to use as poisoned darts. The Indians attempted to lure Cavendish and his men further up the river but, sensing a trap, the Englishmen fired some shots from their arquebuses and returned to their ships.

Now, as they were negotiating the last leg of their passage through the straits, their luck changed, and bad weather forced the ships to seek shelter for a full month. Driving rain and storm-force winds hit them with a violence that put at risk their best anchors and strongest cables. Their only food during this critical period consisted of mussels, limpets and such birds as they could catch on shore.

At long last the winds moderated and on 24 February the flotilla, still intact, entered the Pacific Ocean, or South Sea, as it was then called. Their passage through the straits had taken 49 days, more than three times what it had taken Drake. Cavendish set a course northwards up the west coast of South America, but before they had got very far, they ran into another storm, as bad as any they had so far encountered, in the course of which the *Hugh Gallant* parted company with the other ships. At one point our chronicler on board the bark thought she looked 'every hour to sink, being so leaky, and ourselves so weakened with freeing it from water, that we slept not in three days and three nights'.

After four days the storm abated, but it was not until two weeks later and 1,000 miles further north, near the island of Mocha, off the coast of Chile, that the *Hugh Gallant* rejoined her comrades. Some of the men went ashore on Mocha Island and were immediately set upon by the Indians armed with bows and arrows, much as they had attacked Drake when he had landed there. Unlike Drake and his party, however, Cavendish's men escaped injury and returned to their ships. But the need to water and revictual was urgent, so they weighed anchor and found another island suitable for their purpose. Here, Cavendish landed with some 80 of his men, all armed, and were welcomed ashore by the local Indians who mistook them for Spaniards. These Indians, it appeared, had all been converted to Christianity by their Spanish masters, and proved most helpful when they realised that the visitors were English and hated the Spaniards every bit as much as they did.

Meanwhile, Cavendish had discovered that next to the local church was a row of storehouses filled with barrels of wheat and barley, ready threshed, and 'as fair, clean and every way as good as any we have in England'. There were also barrels of potatoes, dried dog fish and maize: all of it intended to meet the tribute exacted by the Spanish authorities. The English helped themselves to what they needed, as well as to as many pigs and hens as they had salt to preserve. Such good fortune did not come their way that often, and Cavendish showed his appreciation to the Indians by inviting two of their senior tribesmen aboard his ship, where he entertained them with food and wine.

The expedition met with varying adventures on its way up the Spanish seaboard of South America. At one bay in which the squadron rode at anchor, it was spotted by an Indian looking after cattle close to the shore. Warned, no doubt, to look out for the English ships, the man grabbed his horse and rode off to raise the alarm before anyone could stop him. Later, when Cavendish and his men landed from their boat, they saw three mounted soldiers riding towards them. The soldiers halted at a distance from the English pirates. They parleyed and Cavendish agreed to send Fernando, the Spaniard he had picked up in the Magellan Straits, to negotiate for victuals. However, no sooner had Fernando begun talking with the Spanish soldiers than he leaped up behind one of them and off they all rode together, this despite Fernando's 'deep and damnable oathes' which he had made to Cavendish, 'never to forsake him, but to die on his side before he would be false'.

The following day, Cavendish dispatched some three score of his men into the interior to find the local town and sack it. The party marched through an agreeable countryside, well stocked with cattle and horses, 'very wild and unhandled', and the habitat of countless hares, conies, partridges and other game. But of people, or their homes, there was no sign. So, when they saw that their path would be blocked by mountains, the men refreshed themselves with river water, then set off back to the coast by a route which they had reckoned would lead them to the town. Further disappointment awaited them: they saw nothing on the homeward trek except packs of wild dogs. They learnt later that, following Fernando's defection, the English party had been watched by some 200 Spanish horsemen with orders to attack them, but who in the event held back, 'for we marched along in array, and observed good order, whereby we seemed a greater number than we were'.

The following day, 1 April, the Spaniards found renewed courage and ambushed the Englishmen when they went ashore to fill their water butts. Never lacking in courage, Cavendish's men put up a good fight despite the heavy odds against them, killing some 24 of the enemy against a loss of 12 men of their own.

After such rough handling, an agreeable surprise was in store when, on 15 April, they landed at a place called Morro Moreno which stands almost on the Tropic of Capricorn. The Indians of that town gave them a friendly reception and brought them fresh water and wood. Simple, hospitable people, 'in marvellous awe' of the Spaniards, they conducted their visitors to where their women were. Their homes consisted of 'nothing but the skin of a beast laid upon the ground, and over them nothing but five or six sticks laid across, which stand upon two forks with sticks on the ground, and a few boughs laid on top'. Their diet was raw fish which 'stinketh most vilely'. Pretty adds that these Indians also made their canoes out of animal skins, stretched and inflated like bladders, and sewn together by the sinews of wild beasts. Much of the fish which they caught with their primitive gear went to the Spaniards for tribute.

As the English flotilla sailed northwards, Cavendish became bolder in his attacks on Spanish ships and property. On 23 April they were off the port of Arica, where the border of Chile meets that of Peru and the ocean terminal of the Potosi silver mines, which were the greatest single asset of the Spanish empire. They lost no time in capturing two barks and a large ship of 100 tons, riding close into the town but empty. Cavendish decided to keep one of the barks, renaming it the *George*. The large ship he offered back to the Spanish in return for the English prisoners taken earlier in the month, but the Spaniards refused such an exchange, so Cavendish fired the ship and scuttled the other bark.

Meanwhile, the *Content* had parted company with the flotilla in order to capture a cargo of wine which had been landed some miles south of Arica, and rejoined the other ships too late to provide Cavendish with the force he needed to sack the well-fortified town of Arica – an engagement he would not have hesitated to undertake had he been at full strength.

Their course now lay north-west, following the coastline of Peru. News of Cavendish's exploits were beginning to spread, and they intercepted a small bark carrying messages to Lima further north. On board were a Greek pilot, three Spaniards and a Fleming. Not until the thumbscrews were produced, and used, did Cavendish wring from his prisoners that the true purpose of their mission was to give warning to Spanish shipping and ports of the approach of the English privateers.

On 10 May it was once again the turn of the *Hugh Gallant* to part company with her companions. Now alone, she put in at a bay in search of fresh water. It turned out to be a happy choice of watering place, for not only did they find ample water but also an unexpected windfall, for covered with bunches of reeds near the shore was a cache of several hundred bags of meal – a welcome addition to their larder, which was nearly empty. The following day they came across a bark drawn up on the beach, about a cable's length from the water. Not without difficulty they succeeded in launching her, only to find that their prize was little more than a leaky wreck which they had no alternative but to abandon. On 16 May came another change of fortune; this time their prize was a 300-ton ship with a crew of 24, amongst them a Spanish pilot and a black man called Emmanuel, both of whom they took along with them. There was, however, little else worth taking, except a foresail and some victuals, of which they never seemed to have too much.

The stragglers met their admiral again on the following day, when they learnt that, in their absence, Cavendish had taken two worthwhile prizes. The first was laden with sugar, molasses, maize, Cordovan skins, Indian coats, marmalade and hens, the second with wheatmeal and yet more marmalade. The English had helped them-selves to as much of this as they could carry, and put a match to the rest, along with the ships.

On 20 May they arrived off the town of Paita, close to the present frontier between Peru and Ecuador. It was, according to Francis Pretty, a fair-sized town of upwards of 200 houses and a guildhall. After a skirmish, Cavendish took the town with a force of 70 men with the support of the ships' guns. Fearing such an attack, the people had carried their goods and valuables up into the mountains for safe keeping, but it did not take the raiders long to discover their hiding place, and the pickings surpassed their expectations, including 25lbs. of silver pieces of eight and an abundance of household goods. Before returning to their ships, they set fire to the town and to some £6,000-worth of goods, as well as to a Spanish bark riding in the roads outside.

The island of Puna, which lies some 200 miles south of the equator, is favoured with an excellent harbour, which the English discovered for themselves when they arrived five days later. They also discovered, riding at anchor in that harbour, a ship of some 250 tons which they promptly sank. That done, they landed and made for a sumptuous-looking house which evidently belonged to the lord of the island. The rooms were large and stately and commanded fine views of the sea on one side and the island on the other. Underneath was a 'marvellous great hall', at one end of which was a storehouse loaded with materials for making ships' cables, for which the island was locally famous. As for the lord himself, he had received advance warning of Cavendish's approach and fled to the mainland, taking with him his wife and entourage, as well as treasure to the value of 100,000 crowns. This, and other useful information, Cavendish extracted from an Indian who had been sent to spy on the English raiders. The lord, it seemed, was a man of considerable wealth, Indian born but married to a beautiful Spaniard whom the islanders honoured as they would a queen. So grand was she that whenever she ventured abroad she did so in a litter, carried on the shoulders of four slaves, a canopy over her head to protect her from the elements, and attended by a retinue of her gentlewomen and the 'best men' of the island.

Cavendish judged that there was no time to be lost in pursuit of the treasure. Crossing the mainland, his suspicions were alerted by the presence at the landing place of several open boats loaded with provisions, but no sign of anybody aboard them. From the guarded hints dropped by his Indian guide, Cavendish guessed that the boats had brought reinforcements of Spanish soldiers for the defence of the town and shipping.

'Not a whit discouraged' by this information, Cavendish's party pressed on and, under cover of darkness, followed a lonely path in the woods to the house where they expected to catch up with their prey. However, luck was against them as the house was empty. The occupants must have had scant warning of Cavendish's approach for 'they left the meat roasting by the fire and were fled with their treasures'.

Some compensation for their disappointment at the failure of this exploit was provided the next day when Cavendish rowed to another island. Here, the lord of Puna had concealed 'all the hangings of his chambers, which were of Cordovan leather, all gilded over and painted very fair and rich, with all his household stuff, and all the ships' tackle which was riding in the roads at our coming'. The raiding party helped themselves to everything which Cavendish considered requisite, as Master Pretty puts it, 'for the ship's business', including a great quantity of nails and iron spikes.

The Englishmen were clearly impressed by the island of Puna which had 'all things requisite and fruitful' – all things, that is, except gold or silver mines! Pretty judged it to be about the size of the Isle of Wight. The town adjoining the lord's palace contained some 200 houses, perhaps more, and there were at least two other towns on the island as large. Fig trees grew in the palace gardens, along with oranges, lemons,

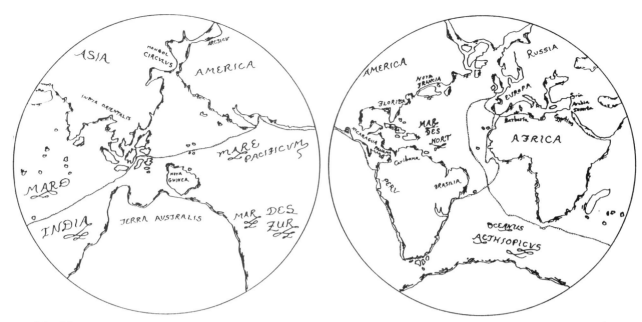

20. The route taken by Thomas Cavendish in his circumnavigation of the globe, taken from a map by the Dutch cartographer Jodocus Hondius, printed *c*.1590.

Aemulus æquorei, admiratorque Draconis
Commodiore via, et spacijs breuioribus Orbem
Circumagens, patriam multa cum laude reuisi:
Pluraque Neptuno et dignißima Marte peregi.
Si Mare Cretensis nescit, tum nesciet Anglus
Oceanum, et viuet positis inglorius armis.

21. Thomas Cavendish. The text in the border reads 'Thomas Candyssh a noble Englishman at the age of thirty', and that beneath the globes, 'let a man be ashamed to turn aside from distant places'. The text beneath the picture translates as: 'I was competing for the same thing and an admirer of the more fortunate Drake on his voyage. In a shorter time, sailing round the world, I returned to my native land with great praise. I accomplished many very creditable deeds on the ocean and in warfare. If an Englishman is ignorant of the Cretan Sea, then he may be ignorant of the ocean and may pass an inglorious life, having laid down his weapons'.

pomegranates and limes. Melons, cucumbers, radishes and herbs also thrived there in abundance.

The lord had been converted to Christianity at the time of his marriage to the Spaniard, and his conversion was followed by that of his subjects. He built a large church close to his palace, where the whole community came to hear mass. The English burnt the church and took the bells away with them.

Retribution for this pointless act of sacrilege was swift. Early on the morning of 2 June some 20 of Cavendish's men were foraging for victuals when they were set upon by 200 Spanish soldiers, well-armed and led by an ensign, who had landed unseen on the other side of the island during the night. Together with a force of as many Indians, armed with bows and arrows, they completely surprised the English party, killing two of them before they could reach the shelter of nearby buildings. 'We skirmished with them for an hour and a half' our chronicler informs us:

> At last being sore overcharged with multitudes, we were driven down from the hill to the water's side, and there kept them at bay for a while, until, in the end, Zachery Saxie, who with his halberd had kept the way of the hill and slain a couple of them, was himself shot in the heart and, crying to God for mercy, fell down dead.

Pretty and his companions continued to give a good account of themselves until their boat came and took off as many as it could carry, returning for the others later. Casualties were high on both sides – 46 Spaniards and 12 English – five were killed by the enemy, one by his own piece accidentally, one was burnt, two drowned (including Ambrose the musician) and three taken prisoner.

Cavendish returned to the attack with a stronger force and this time the English got the better of their enemy who gave ground. This done, they set fire to the town and to four ships being built on the stocks, and afterwards 'made havoc of their fields, orchards and gardens'. The next day, 3 June, in defiance of the Spaniards, they graved and trimmed two of their own ships and two days later, all being ready, sailed northwards out of the Puna roads. It had been an eventful 11 days.

Due to losses, there were no longer enough of them to man all the ships, a problem which Cavendish solved by sinking the *Hugh Gallant*. This they did, not, one assumes, without feelings of regret for those who, like Francis Petty, had sailed in her for almost a year, at a place called Rio Dolce. They crossed the equator on 12 June and continued on the same course all that month, putting the fear of God into the hearts of all those who lived and traded along the coast. Although now in command of a smaller force, Cavendish did not abate his attacks upon Spanish property.

From one of the ships which they fired they took on board a pilot whose knowledge and experience was likely to be useful. His name was Michael Sanctius, a Provençal born in Marseilles. In addition to information about shipping along that part of the coast, the Frenchman whispered to Cavendish news of a great Spanish treasure ship, the *Santa Anna*, on her way across the South Sea from the Philippines with a full hold – just the kind of prize the Englishmen had been praying for since the day they left Plymouth Sound! Meanwhile, Cavendish could use some more hands so, along with Michael Sanctius and some sails and ropes, he took over the crew of six before firing their ship.

By 27 July, they were running along the coast of Guatemala. Here they sacked the town of Aguatulco and found in the customs house some 600 bags of anil dye and 400 bags of cacaos which, Pretty writes, were 'very like unto an almond, but nothing so pleasant in taste. They eat them and make a drink of them'. We do so still and call it chocolate.

Cavendish and his men had been at sea a full 12 months and were by now running up the coast of Mexico, having 'overslipped the haven of Acapulco', probably inadvertently, because it was from that port that Spanish ships sailed for the Philippines. On the other hand, Cavendish may have been husbanding his resources for what he hoped might be the climax to his voyages.

In the meantime, they intercepted another courtier, this time a mullato, carrying letters warning of the danger to Spanish property from the English raiders. They fished for pearls, and the constant need for water and victuals was ever an important part of the pattern of life. Pretty reported that they killed seals and iguanas which were 'very good meat'.

By 24 September they had reached Mazatlan, just south of the Tropic of Cancer, some 200 miles east of the tip of the Californian peninsula. Their first need as always, and particularly in those latitudes, was water. Unable to take it on here because at low tide the river mouth was shoaled, they moved on to an island a league to the north. Here they had to dig for water, after one of their Spanish prisoners, a water diviner, showed them the place. They stayed some 10 days on this island, trimming their ships and rebuilding their pinnace. Then, on 9 October, they sailed westward to the Cape of San Lucas on the point of California, reaching the cape – 'very like the Needles on the Isle of Wight' – five days later. They watered in the river which flowed into the bay of Aguada Segura and lay off the cape of San Lucas until 4 November, almost as if Cavendish was waiting to keep a rendezvous he was determined not to miss. These was a growing sense of expectation, not to say tension, amongst the men.

'A sail! A sail!' shouted the look-out from the mast top. He was the ship's trumpeter and his voice was heard joyfully by the whole company, who raised a mighty cheer. He had sighted the prize they had been waiting for, the great treasure ship that was carrying King Philip's gold – the 700-ton *Santa Anna*.

After the sighting had been confirmed by the master of the ship and 'divers others of the company' who also went up into the main top to see for themselves, Cavendish ordered them to 'put all things in readiness' and, this done, they set off in hot pursuit of their prey. The wind was in their favour and, after some three hours, they overtook the Spaniard and fired a broadside into her, together with a volley of small shot. For an eye-witness's account of the battle, we quote Francis Pretty:

Now, as we were ready on their ship's side to board her, being not past fifty or sixty men on our ship, we perceived that the captain of the Spaniard had made 'fights' fore and after, and laid their sails close on their poop, mid-ship and fo'castle, and having not one man to be seen, stood close upon their fights with lances, javelins, rapiers and innumerable great stones, which they threw overboard upon our heads and into our ship so fast that they put us off their ship again, with the loss of two of our men, slain, and the wounding of four or five.

But for all this, we retrimmed our sails and gave them a fresh encounter with our great ordnance, and also with our small shot, raking them through and through, to the killing and maiming of many of their men. Their captain, still like a valiant man, with his company stood very stoutly unto his close fights, not yielding as yet. Our general encouraged his men afresh with the whole noise of trumpets, and we gave them the third encounter with our great ordnance and all our small shot, to the great discomforting of our enemies, raking them through in divers places, killing and spoiling many of their men. The enemy, after five or six hours fight, their ship being in hazard of sinking, set out a flag of truce and parleyed for mercy, desiring our general to save their lives and to take their goods, and that they would presently yield ...

Thus was the mighty *Santa Anna*, pride of the Spanish fleet in the South Sea, taken by the English privateers. The ship was laden with 22,000 pesos-worth of gold, rich furnishings such as satin, silks and damasks, spices, preserves and other choice foodstuffs and wines. The ship's company, some 190 Spaniards all told, were put ashore with an ample supply of food, water and wine, and the victors got down to the serious business of dividing the spoils. There was some disagreement amongst them. For a time mutiny was threatened, expecially by those on board the *Content* who felt they had a raw deal, but Cavendish managed to preserve the peace, at least for the time being.

The *Santa Anna* was carrying a small number of people who Cavendish decided, for one reason or another, to take along with him. There were two young men from Japan, three from Manila, a Portuguese who had been in China, Japan and the Philippines, and a Spanish pilot familiar with the route across the Pacific which Cavendish planned to take on his way home to England.

The anniversary of Queen Elizabeth's coronation fell on 17 November and, in celebration, the English ships fired their guns and, after darkness fell, let off many fireworks. Two days later, they set fire to the *Santa Anna*, together with such of her cargo which they could not find room for, and the English 'set sail joyfully homewards with a fair wind ...'.

Almost immediately the *Desire* and *Content* lost touch with each other, whether by accident or design following the disagreement after the share-out is not stated. The fact remains that Cavendish never saw the *Content* or her ship's company again.

Following a similar route across the Pacific as Drake, they reached, after 45 days at sea, an island in the Ladrones group. Cavendish experienced the same difficulty with the natives as had both his predecessors, Magellan and Drake. As soon as they dropped anchor, they were surrounded by scores of canoes loaded with produce, which the natives offered to the Englishmen in exchange for artefacts. This bartering was fun for a time, but the natives were so importunate that they would not leave, until in the end the English were driven to fire at them.

Compared with the adventures of the outward voyage, the return journey must have seemed something of an anti-climax – long stretches of open sea unrelieved by the anticipation of landing a good prize when they reached port. On 14 January they sighted Manila in the Philippines. This was an important port for Spanish ships trading with China and South America, and some 700 Spaniards lived there.

In February, an outbreak of fever hit the ship's company. Captain Havers, one of Cavendish's senior officers, went down with the illness, as did Francis Pretty. He ascribed it to the 'extreme heat and intemperate climate'. Captain Havers died of the infection, 'to the no small grief of our general and of all the rest of the company', and was buried at sea. Pretty recovered.

On 1 March they dropped anchor off the south-west coast of Java, whose king was happy to supply them with provisions. Several canoes laden with victuals arrived, including two live oxen, 10 pigs, countless hens, ducks, geese, eggs, bananas, sugar canes, coconuts, oranges and much else besides. On the island were two Portuguese factors whom Cavendish made a point of meeting. The two factors found a warm welcome awaiting them on the English ship, for they were the first friendly Europeans they had spoken to in 18 months. Cavendish gave his guests the news that Spain was at war with England. In return for news about their king, Don Antonio, the Portuguese said that Java was rich in natural produce, as well as merchandise. They added that the king in that part of the island was a man much feared by his subjects, and that he was also a man great in years and had 100 wives. When he died, he would be cremated and his ashes preserved. According to custom, his wives would assemble at an appointed place within five days of the king's death. The favourite wife would pick up a ball and throw it, and at the place where the ball fell, each wife would stab herself to death.

The *Desire* took her leave of Java on 16 March and set a course for the Cape of Good Hope which they rounded some two months later. On 9 June, they anchored off the pleasant and congenial island of St Helena, and here they rested for 11 days before setting sail for what was to be the last leg of their voyage home. On 3 September they received important news from a Flemish ship just out of Lisbon – England had defeated the great Spanish Armada! There was 'singular rejoicing' at this stirring news.

Francis Pretty ends his chronicle of Thomas Cavendish's voyage of circumnavigation in these words: 'the 9 September, after a terrible tempest which carried away most part of our sails, by the merciful favour of the Almighty, we recovered our long-wished for port of Plymouth in England, from whence we set forth at the beginning of our voyage'. Of the original complement of 123 men, only 50 returned, amongst whom was Thomas Eldred. When the *Desire* sailed up the Thames, eyewitnesses recorded that 'all her mariners and sailors were clothed in silk, her sails of damask, and her topmasts cloth of gold'. In 1591 Captain Cavendish embarked on another round-the-world voyage which ended in disaster; he died and was buried at sea, probably in May 1592.

Thomas Eldred spent his remaining years in Ipswich. A document dated 21 June 1603, about the Brooke Street property where he and his family had lived for many years, refers to 'Thomas Eldred, late of Ipswich, Chandler, and wife, Margery, deceased', his burial is not recorded in the St Clement's church register, but he and his wife were probably buried there. It is said that there was once a banner commemorating his epic achievement suspended in the church.

22. Oak mantelpiece originally in the
Eldred house on Fore Street, Ipswich
(*above*), and now (*right*) in Christchurch
Mansion. The panel paintings portray
Thomas Eldred, a globe (the emblem of a
circumnavigation) and a ship, possibly
the *Desire*.

There may also have been a monument, as an old news article on the church reads in part:

> the stone that marked the spot has or had this inscribed upon it, for we have not been able to discover it: 'He that travels ye world about seeth God's wonders and God's works. Thomas Eldred travelled ye world about; and went out of Plimouth ye 21 of July 1586, and arrived in Plimouth again the 9 of September 1588'.

Among relics from the Eldred House on Fore Street now at the Christchurch Mansion in Ipswich is the handsome mantelpiece with its three paintings – the ship on the left, the globe in the centre, and the portrait of a middle-aged man holding a telescope or navigating instrument on the right. The above inscription appears under the centre panel. These paintings were made in the early 17th century and probably belonged to Thomas' son, also Thomas, and also an Ipswich merchant. A second group of panel paintings was in the possession of John Eldred, son of Thomas the Mariner and owner of Olivers Manor near Colchester in Essex. In the Olivers paintings there was a ship on the left, a portrait of an elderly man in the centre and a globe on the right. Under the globe was inscribed 'Thomas Eldred went out of Plimmouthe 1586 July 21 and sailed about the whole globe and arrived again in Plimmouthe ye 9 of September 1588. What can seeme greate to him that hath seene the whole world and the wondrous works therein, save the Maker of it and the world above it'. The elderly man is holding an astrolabe that is clearly marked with the date 1620. This date on the Olivers painting is mysterious. Is the portrait that of Thomas Eldred the Mariner? Is the date in error or is it the year in which the painting was completed?

There were several Thomas Eldreds in Ipswich and elsewhere in Suffolk and vicinity during the 16th and 17th centuries. For example, there was a Thomas who died in 1587, while Thomas the Mariner left a son Thomas (1561-1624) who was a merchant like his father. This Thomas mentions in his will a nephew, Thomas Eldred, son of his deceased brother William (1572-1624). This last Thomas (c.1595-1640) may have been the one mentioned in Ipswich records 'in command of a ship lately come from Denmark' in 1625 (*Dictionary of National Biography*). Records show that a Thomas Eldred was buried at Great Saxham on 5 November 1622. Some believe that he may have been Thomas Eldred the Mariner, but it is most likely that he was a close relative of John Eldred the Traveller who is also buried here.

As previously stated, we do not know who the parents of Thomas Eldred the Mariner were. Many Eldred family genealogists believe that he was the youngest son of Nicholas (1496-1566) and Bridget Eldred of Knettisall. The will of Nicholas, dated 27 August 1566, is on file at the Suffolk Record Office, Bury St Edmunds (reference Arnold 366). It mentions his wife Bridget, his father Thomas Eldred of Knettisall, his son William of Knettisall, his sons Thomas and Edmund of Ipswich, and his daughter Allyce, wife to Stephen Roockewood. However, Nicholas does not say in his will that his son Thomas in Ipswich is married and has four children which Thomas the Mariner did have in August 1566. Furthermore, a son of Thomas the Mariner mentions his uncle, Philip, living at Hadleigh in 1623 whom Nicholas does not name

Philip as one of his three sons. In summary, there is much to be learned about Thomas Eldred – his parents, early life and life after his remarkable voyage. There is little doubt that he had a great-grandson, Samuel Eldred (1620-*c*.1697), who was an early emigrant to America. It is interesting to note that Samuel inherited from his father the 'great sea-chest that my father, William Eldred of Bury, had from his father, Thomas Eldred, the one who sailed around the world'.

John Eldred sailed on the *Hercules*.

Chapter Seven

William Eldred of Dover Castle, Dover, (c.1563-after 1646)

William was one of three members of the Eldred family whose achievements were sufficiently distinguished to merit inclusion in the *Dictionary of National Biography*. The others were John Eldred, the merchant adventurer of the City of London and Great Saxham in Suffolk, and Thomas Eldred, sea captain and ship's chandler of Ipswich, whose most noteworthy exploit was to sail around the world with Thomas Cavendish. All three men lived during the second half of the 16th century and the first half of the 17th century. Genealogists have not yet established their relationship to each other.

We know little of the personal details of William's life – where he was born, who his parents were, whether he married or if he had children. We do know that he was born *c*.1563 and that, like his two famous kinsmen, he had a long life. There is no record of his death nor of his burial place – presumably it would have been in Dover where he lived and worked for most of his life.

By profession William Eldred was a gunner, but he also had a creative streak in his nature; otherwise, posterity would have had nothing to remember him by except his signature as a freeholder of Dover on the Kentish petition in 1641 for the reformation of the Liturgy. As it was, he left two works of great technical and historical interest. One was a book on gunnery and the other, not mentioned in the *Dictionary of National Biography*, was a series of hand-drawn maps comprising a complete survey of the port of Dover in the early part of the 17th century.

His book, entitled *The Gunner's Glasse, Wherein the Diligent Practitioner May See His Defects, and May, From Point to Point, Reform and Amend All Errors that are Commonly Incident to Unskilful Gunners*, was published in 1646 when the author was about 83 years old. His survey of Dover, which has been described as 'such a perfect record of its middle state that the town may well be proud of possessing', was completed five years earlier. A copy of *The Gunner's Glasse* with a portrait of William on the title page is in the British Library. The *Survey of Dover* is carefully stored in the archives of the Dover Harbour Board where it is available for inspection.

It is evident from these two works that William Eldred was an industrious and painstaking man. As a young gunner he served in France, the Netherlands and Germany before settling in Dover where he lived for 60 years. Here he was appointed to the important position of Master Gunner of Dover Castle. He was apparently satisfactory in this post as he was also made Master Gunner of the Cinque Ports. He kept careful notes of all matters relating to his profession and these he embodied in his treatise on gunnery, the publication of which he justified by saying that 'it is better to furnish a fort with traitors than with unskilled gunners' – a view which is no doubt as valid today as it was in William's time. He dedicated the work to the Earl of Warwick, adding the following verse:

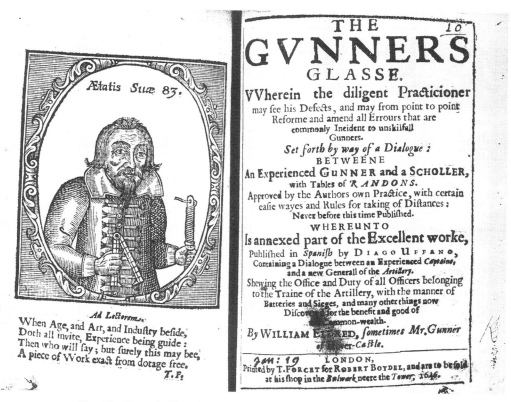

23. *The Gunner's Glasse* by William Eldred, published in 1646.

When age and art and industry beside
Doth all invite, experience being guide,
Then who will say but surely this may be
A piece of work exact from dotage free.

It was probably because of William's proven industry that the formidable task of surveying the port of Dover came his way. The last man to have done this was Thomas Cavendish, none other than the captain with whom Thomas Eldred had sailed around the world. At the time of William's commission (1606), King James I had transferred the responsibility for running the port from the Corporation to 'eleven discreet men' called 'the Guardian or Warden and Assistants of the Harbour of Dover'.

William set about measuring and recording in plan form all the new grants of land on the waterfront that had become available after the port had been placed in the hands of commissioners. For each plot he recorded the name of its tenant or tenants. He did this in 1606 and again in 1640. Also, he prepared a general plan of Dover harbour, town and castle, and collected all of these plans into book form. He had 10 pages (five sheets) of large-scale plans of the harbour lands, drawn to a scale of 48 ft. to one inch. These, with the general plan of the town, are an important historical record for the area covered.

The finished work was dedicated to the Duke of Richmond who was Lord Warden of the Cinque Ports from 1640 until Dover came under the jurisdiction of the Parliamentarians in 1642. In a somewhat fulsome dedication, typical of the period in which he lived, William wrote that he presented his book 'unto all this honourable sessions which now are, and always have been, so careful for the benefit of the harbour, to the intent it may remain to succeeding ages, which will be then in more use than it is now ...'. (The dedication is given in full in *Appendix IV.*)

How right William was in that remark! Today Dover is one of the largest passenger ports in the world, and it is gratifying to know that a member of the Eldred family played a significant role in its history.

Chapter Eight

Olivers and the Eldreds of Essex

Outstanding, mainly Georgian house, set in an exceptional parkland position and enjoying southerly views over the Roman River Valley. Superb, immaculately restored accommodation and beautiful, landscaped gardens.

Such were the glowing terms in which Olivers, home of five generations of the Eldred family, was advertised for sale in the summer of 1980. Indeed, the event was thought to be of sufficient local interest to warrant a report in the *Essex County Standard* of 9 May. Under the headline 'Manor for Sale', the house was described as 'one of the most magnificent and most expensive' in the Colchester area. As to the price, 'a figure in the region of between £225,000 and £250,000' was being sought for the property.

Of the original 15th-century building only a part in the rear of the house survives from the time when John Eldred of Colchester, merchant, alderman and Justice of the Peace, bought it 350 years ago from Thomas Nawnton. The Nawntons had owned it for some years. After the house was severely damaged by fire in the mid-18th century, the front and south elevations were rebuilt in the formal style of the period. The enchanting setting, however, cannot have changed much over the centuries even though it is only about two miles from the centre of Colchester.

Olivers is in a historic corner of England, and Colchester is a historic town – the first in Britain to be mentioned in written sources. Once the capital of King Cunobelin (Shakespeare's Cymbeline), it became an important Roman settlement where 11 British kings surrendered to Emperor Claudius. Later, it was sacked by Queen Boadicea, retaken by the Romans and later occupied, in turn, by the Saxons and Danes. And it was in Colchester that the Normans built their largest castle keep, most of which, along with the Roman city walls and other historic buildings, still stands. Incidentally, there is a street in Colchester today called Eldred Avenue.

The original Eldred owner of Olivers was John, a younger son of Thomas Eldred, tallow-chandler and mariner of Ipswich in Suffolk. John, like most ambitious younger sons, left home to seek his fortune elsewhere. His father was to earn for himself a place in English history when he accompanied Thomas Cavendish of Trimley on a round-the-world voyage of discovery from 1586-88. Meanwhile, the young John travelled up the London road as far as Colchester, a town some 16 miles south of Ipswich. There he became a merchant, probably in the cloth trade which had been established in the town in the Middle Ages and was to expand greatly in the 17th century with the help of Flemish refugees.

John ('John I' to distinguish him from his linear descendants of the same name) prospered in his chosen trade and, in time, became a wealthy man. He was active in local affairs. Like his brothers, Thomas at Ipswich and Philip at Hadleigh, he became bailiff (later called mayor) of his adopted town, first in 1609 and then in 1623.

24.   The 18th-century frontage of Olivers in 1982.

Long before such honours came his way, John married Elizabeth Rusham of London. The wedding took place at St Leonard's church in that part of town known as the Hythe – evidently the merchants' quarter, as it was there that the ships, then and now, load and discharge their cargoes. The church is still there, famous for its fine old hammerbeam roof which has remained as it was when John and Elizabeth exchanged their vows all those years ago.

The exact size of their family is unknown. Some records indicate that there were four children, others seven. Undoubtedly the apogee of John's career occurred in 1634 when, to borrow the formal language of the College of Arms:

the Heralds pursuant to royal commission, made the Visitation of the County of Essex and recognised, as regards the Eldreds of Colchester, a right to Arms and Crest coming to them by virtue of the issue of Letters Patent of Sir Richard St George, Clarenceaux King of Arms, 14th February, 1630, to John Eldred of Colchester.

The tallow-chandler's son had come a long way. Now a man of substance and importance, he had definitely joined the élite ranks of the local gentry. In keeping with such a position, he acquired a country house, Olivers, at Stanway, and another, Little Birch Hall, in the village of Birch, where his eldest daughter, Mary, lived with her husband John Brand. Both houses were within easy reach of Colchester. John outlived his wife and spent his declining years at Little Birch, dying there in 1646 at the age of eighty-one. He was buried in the parish church but, when that building began to fall down, was re-interred in St Andrew's, Earls Colne, a village to the west of Colchester where a memorial was erected to him and to the four successive John Eldreds of Colchester.

John II, who, we assume, went to live at Olivers when his father moved to Little Birch Hall, had the benefit of a good education. He was admitted as a Fellow Commoner to Peterhouse College, Cambridge, in 1621, and two years later was at Lincoln's Inn. He became a Justice of the Peace like his father, and in 1645 he was a Collector of Sequestrations for the county. About this time, according to Morant, he was also employed on 'several other affairs', but what these affairs were Morant does not say. We do know that he supported Parliament during the Civil War and held local office during the Interregnum when Oliver Cromwell ruled.

John married Anne Godman (sometimes spelt Goodman), daughter of Thomas Godman, a lawyer of the Middle Temple whose home was in Leatherhead in Surrey, an agreeable dormitory town south of London. She bore him eight children, all of whom survived, and when she died in 1678, four years before her husband, she was commemorated by a special memorial medal struck by her family. The following description of this medal is adapted from an article in *Medallic Illustrations of British History* (1885):

> on the obverse side is the armorial shield granted John Eldred of Colchester on 14 February 1630 – azure, a cross patée fitchée or, on the chief of the last three globes of the first, impaling Godman per pale ermine and ermines, on a chief indented or, a lion passant vert. Round the edge of the medal on the same side is the legend: Anne, the wife of Jo. Eldred Esq. Died Mar. the 31st 1678, Aged 72. On the reverse side is a veiled female figure seated, facing, holding a skull, and resting her head upon her hand, supported by a pedestal on which stands an urn. The legend reads: A wise woman buildeth her house. The description goes on to point out that the medal is very rare of its kind, that it is cast, chased, high relief and of rather coarse workmanship. It is also hollow, as distinct from another specimen in the British Museum which is solid.

The medal so described was purchased at Sotheby's in 1907 by a London collector, Sir John Evans; the following year Lady Evans, his wife, contributed an article to the *Numismatic Chronicle* in which she had some interesting comments to make about her husband's acquisition. She wrote:

The motto, 'A woman buildeth her home', is adapted from Proverbs XIV i, and suggests a provident disposition on the part of the lady. Looking at her own position as heiress (she was co-heiress of her father's estate), and the good marriages made by her descendants, it no doubt represents the truth. Such texts were in great favour by Puritan families in her day. The medal is one of a most interesting class referring to domestic events. Such medals indicate, as in this case, a prevalence of good art in simple matters, more common 200 years ago than now, and the consideration of them opens chinks through which we may peep at domestic life in England in the 17th century.

Sir John Ruggles-Brise Bart., of Spains Hall, Finchingfield, Essex, formerly Lord Lieutenant of the county, is distantly connected with the Eldred family and inherited a fine specimen of the Anne Eldred medal, his being of solid silver. In 1964 he exhibited this in a collection of works of art from local houses. The medal was subsequently stolen from Sir John's lovely old Tudor home and has not yet been traced.

John II died in 1682 and was buried at Earls Colne. His eldest son, John III, lived longer than other Eldreds of Olivers and was the most able and interesting. He was the only member of the family to sit in Parliament. John III was born in Colchester on 2 October 1629, 'at ye house over against ye *King's Head*'. It was at this same hostelry – the building still stands – that the surrender of Royalist-held Colchester to the Parliamentary forces under Sir Thomas Fairfax was signed during the Civil War after a bitter 12-week siege. That was in 1648, the year that John was admitted at Lincoln's Inn. He had already attended three schools and a university – Colchester, Bishop's Stortford and Merchant Taylor's School in London, then Caius College, Cambridge. He was called to the Bar in 1654.

He held offices in the municipalities of Colchester and Harwich, a seaport 19 miles north-east of Colchester, where he was made a freeman in 1673. He probably joined his father on the Essex commission of the peace after the Restoration in 1660. Both served as pall-bearers at the re-interment of the Cavalier martyr Sir Charles Lucas who, with Sir George Lisle, commanded the king's forces at Colchester. After the surrender both officers were shot in the castle bailey by the Roundheads.

Nevertheless, John III, a dissenter, was clearly no friend of the restored monarchy under Charles II. He became deputy recorder at Colchester and then at Harwich, and sat regularly at the Quarter Sessions from 1660-85. In 1689 he defeated Samuel Pepys at the polls, and was returned to the Convention Parliament as the member for Harwich. At Westminster John was a moderately active member but made no recorded speeches.

John had a personal grievance against James II, who succeeded his elder brother, Charles II, on the throne, when the king took over some of his property in London and Surrey as crown lands. However, in 1688 the king's agents recommended that John be restored to the commission of the peace, a position of which he had been deprived some years before on the grounds that he was an exclusionist. By 1695, when he was 66 years of age, we find his name on documents as one of His Majesty's Deputy Lieutenants of the County of Essex.

So much for his public life, lived at a particularly eventful and probably, for a man of conscience, difficult period in English history. Thanks largely to his practice of keeping a diary of family events, such as births, marriages and deaths, something of

25.   The 16th-century elevation of Olivers in 1982.

his personal life is also known. For instance, the first entry following that of his own birth reads '15 December 1657. I married Margaret Harlackenden'. The entry is corroborated by the marriage register of St Andrew's church, Earls Colne, where the bride had been baptised 22 years earlier.

Some six weeks before the wedding the young bride-to-be went to London on a shopping trip to buy her trousseau. We do not know whether her mother went with her, but the expedition was reported to the Rev. Ralph Jocelyn, a puritanical divine and friend of the family who noted Margaret's extravagance in his own diary – '17 November 1657. Margaret Harlackenden laid out £120 at London for wedding clothes. Her father is angry'. Well might he have been! Three hundred years ago £120 was a small fortune to spend on clothes, even a wedding trousseau!

Not that her father had occasion to stint his daughter, for Colonel Richard Harlackenden of Colne Priory was a wealthy man but came from thrifty stock. Born in 1610, he was High Sheriff of Essex in 1647 and commanded a regiment on the Parliamentary side at the siege of Colchester. His extensive estates were inherited, having originally been purchased in 1583 by his grandfather, Roger Harlackenden, from Edward de Vere, 17th Earl of Oxford, one of the contenders for the authorship of Shakespeare's works. Roger was, in fact, Lord Oxford's steward, but the nobleman was an incorrigible spendthrift. In contrast, Roger was careful and saved his money, eventually paying Lord Oxford £2,000 for the manor and park of Earls Colne – lands that had been granted to the first Earl by William the Conqueror.

For the de Vere family, it was a sad day. They ranked among the oldest and noblest families in all England and were Earls of Oxford from 1137 to 1703 when the male line failed. Lady Diana de Vere, the beautiful daughter of the 20th and last Earl of Oxford, married the 1st Duke of St Albans, natural son of Charles II by Nell Gwynn. Kneller's stunning portrait of her hangs in the King's First Presence Chamber at Hampton Court Palace. Since that time, the name and dignity of the Earls of Oxford have been assumed by successive generations of Beauclerks (the family name of the Dukes of St Albans) who have prefixed 'de Vere' to their own surname and quartered the de Vere arms thus: 'quarterly gules and or, in the first quarter a mullet of five points argent'.

The village of Earls Colne is named after its original owners, the Earls of Oxford, and the flint parapet on the tower of the parish church where John and Margaret were married is studded with the five-pointed star of the de Veres and with their arms in bold relief. It is to one of the inside walls in the nave of this church that the brass memorial to the Eldreds of Olivers is fixed. The connection between the Norman family of de Vere and the Saxon family of Eldred has been revived recently. The present Duke of St Albans is Murray Charles de Vere Beauclerk who, according to *Burke's Peerage*, is the stepson of John Trevor Eldrid of London.

But back to the winter of 1657 and to the wedding of John III who probably had more immediate matters to think about than the decline and fall of the de Veres, although the fact that his wife was co-heiress of what had once been a de Vere estate would surely not have escaped his legal mind. Colonel Harlackenden's anger over his daughter's extravagance did not extend to his future son-in-law, of whom he clearly approved. He made this note in his diary after the ceremony:

> I married my daughter Margaret unto John Eldred Esq., the son of John Eldred Esq., of Stanway, in the county of Essex, with whom I gave £2,000 portion. My son-in-law is a pritty [sic] lawyer, a barrister of two or three years standing, and pleadeth. The marriage was carried very quietly and piously, on no difference on no side, but much love and hearty entertain, and much welcome at both houses. The Lord has much heard and answered my prayers in this business, for I feared my daughter would have done much worse.

From that time on, the ties of common interest and affection which bound the two families at Olivers and Colne Priory grew stronger. To their shared belief in the causes of Puritanism and parliamentary government was added a shared aspiration for the next generation of Eldreds. There was much coming and going between the two houses. Most of John and Margaret's six children were born and baptized at Colne Priory. John's mother died there, whereas Margaret's mother died at Olivers, both in the same year, 1678. Colonel Harlackenden predeceased her by a year. All of these events were carefully noted in John's diary.

John lived to a great age and seemingly enjoyed a strong constitution for on 27 March 1665, he notes, 'A stone was taken out of my bladder by cutting, and in fourteen days the wound was healed'. This operation had been successfully carried out some years earlier on Samuel Pepys. In the same year (1665) London was stricken by the plague which claimed the lives of tens of thousands of its citizens and sent the rich fleeing into the country to escape the infection. Colchester was one of the ports that benefited from the embargo on London imposed by those who were afraid to trade in the capital. In the following year most of London was destroyed in the Great Fire.

We do not know where John was during these disasters, but we do know that he lived to see the marriage of his children, the birth of his grandchildren, and the death of his eldest daughter, Elizabeth, who died in Westminster of smallpox – a common killer in those days. She was buried in St Margaret's, the church that stands in the shadow of Westminster Abbey and which later became the scene of many society weddings. The penultimate entry in John's diary is dated 27 January 1713, and reads 'My wife died and was buried in Earls Colne'.

John survived her by three and a half years, dying at Earls Colne on 2 September 1717 in his 88th year. (The entries in the family diary appear to have been continued by John IV.) His memorial inscription reads: 'John Eldred of Olivers Esq., who, for his extensive knowledge of the Law, his strong attachment to Religion and Virtue, and zealous opposition to Popery and arbitrary government (having a voice in the Convention Parliament) was justly esteemed'.

Olive Eldred, one of John's sisters, whose death he noted in 1697, deserves more than a passing mention in this chronicle, if only on account of the interesting family into which she married. At the time of her death, Olive was the widow of Dr. Thomas Arris, of Hall Place, St Albans, Hertfordshire, the son of a London surgeon, Edward Arris – perhaps the very man who operated to remove the stone in John's bladder.

Dr. Thomas Arris had a notable career. He sat as a member of Parliament for the borough of St Albans in 1661 and was for several years a Justice of the Peace for Hertfordshire. In 1682 he excused himself from attending on account of the gout and was appointed by special brief to receive contributions for the repair of St Albans' Abbey. He was also one of the 'worshipful company' which attended the performance of a play in 1662 given by the boys of St Albans' Grammar School. The play was called *Lingua,* or ye *Combatte Between ye Tongue and ye Five Senses.* In 1908, almost 250 years later, the same play was re-enacted by the boys of the school, and one of the minor parts was performed by 'Master James Eldred' whose family was then living in the city.

In the church of St Sepulchre, at the north-east corner of Holborn viaduct in the City of London, one of the few city churches to survive both the Great Fire and the 'Blitz', there is a remarkable monument to Thomas Arris's parents, Edward and Mary. The memorial consists of two effigies, presumably portraits from life, and under each is an inscription. Edward's reads:

Edward Arris Esqr. gave to the Company of Chyrurgeons £30 for an anatomy lecture and to the Hospital of St Bartholomew £24, both yearly forever; to Christ Church Hospital £100, and £50 toward rebuilding of this church; and several large gifts to the poor of this parish, wherein he was born, and all these in his lifetime. He deceased the 28th May 1676, aged 85 and lyeth buryed by his wife.

Mary's inscription, alongside that of her husband, reads:

> Neer this place lyeth inter'd the body of Mary Arris ye wife of Edward Arris Esqr and sometime Alderman of this City. They were married 60 years and had issue 23 children whereof only Thomas Arris (Dr. in Physick, fellow of the College in London, Justice of ye Peace in the County of Hartford and a member of the Honble. House of Commons) her survived. She dyed ye 11th of Dec. 1674 aged 76 years.

John IV was born in 1666, the year of the Great Fire of London. His father notes: 'My second son, John, was born at Earls Colne and baptised the same day'. His first son, John, had been born three years earlier but died in infancy, 'and was buried in ye chancell at Earls Colne'. In those days, infant mortality was such that, whenever possible, babies were born and baptised on the same day.

We know less about John IV than we do about John III, although we do know what he looked like from a contemporary portrait in the possession of the author of this article of London, England. He was married in the chapel at Lincoln's Inn in 1702 to Mary Horsman. Her father, Robert Horsman, was a lawyer and came from Stretton in Rutland. Their first-born was a son. John III wrote: '13 Dec. 1703. My grandson, John Horsman Eldred, was born at Olivers and baptized the same day, but dyed 2nd February following'. Two years later, Mary was delivered of another boy; he survived and became John V, last in the direct male line of the Eldreds of Olivers.

Of John and Mary's three daughters only Anne, born in 1708, married; both Dulcibella and Mary died in 1736. Anne's husband was John Wale who inherited Colne Priory through his mother, sister of the last Richard Harlackenden. The relationships between the Eldreds, Harlackendens and other Essex families with whom they were connected are confusing and sometimes difficult to untangle. The intermarriage of cousins may have helped to keep their estates within their respective families, but it would also have had the effect of weakening the strain.

John IV died in November 1732 aged 66, and was buried alongside his kinsmen at Earls Colne. His widow and 'mournful relict', as she described herself, inscribed these words on his monument: '[his] humanity and genrous [sic] sentiments of liberty, Religious and Civil, shew to the world how little he deviated from the merit of his ancestors'.

What of the last Eldred master of Olivers? John V married Susanna, fourth daughter of Samuel Rawstorn of Lexden, a village on the outskirts of Colchester. They had no children and no information has yet come to light concerning their life together. John died in 1738, only six years after his father and in the same year as his 'dear mother' whom he survived by only a few months. She was 62 years of age, he only thirty-three. Susanna, John's widow, lived on in the house for another 40 years, after which Olivers passed, via John's aunt Mary Barfoot, through the female line into the ownership of the Harrison family, who held it until shortly before the Second World War. Many of the Harrisons were parsons, and one was Bishop of Glasgow; few of them lived at Olivers, as they preferred to rent it to tenants.

26. John Eldred ('John IV') of Olivers (1666-1732).

27. Portrait of Mary Eldred, wife of John, by Michael Dahl (1656-1743). This painting was purchased by John Trevor Eldrid in 1978.

In his history of Essex, Philip Morant describes Olivers as he found it in the middle of the 18th century, presumably while Susanna Eldred still lived there:

> The mansion house stands about two miles south-east of Stanway church in a retired but agreeable place, with handsome gardens, canals and fishponds; and a wood opening out with pleasant walks. It took its name from a family named Oliver. John, son of Ralph, who was the son of Oliver, lived here in the reign of King Henry III and, in the thirteenth year of the reign of King Edward, he claimed certain land in Stanway of the abbot of Colchester.

Olivers passed through several hands before John Eldred I bought it 'about the beginning' of the 17th century. Morant lists the families of Durward, Knivet and Nawnton amongst those who owned the manor before the Eldreds, and there may well have been others. The Harrisons leased the house to tenants; being a rather impecunious family, they sometimes let the place fall into a state of neglect bordering on dilapidation. There was, for instance, the occasion when Mr. Steinman, a contributor to the *Gentleman's Magazine*, visited Olivers in 1831 and was shocked by its condition. He found the exterior of the house 'in no way striking save in its fearful state of repair', which suggested to him that in a very few more years 'it would be no more'. 'It is a low, long brick pile, with modern windows', he went on, 'the room, once a library, has fallen entirely down as has a great part of the parapet on one side; and the ceiling of the great dining room is sustained only by two rudely-squared stems of trees placed under the beam'.

Mr. Steinman observed that the house stood on a manor embracing more than 327 acres. He learned that when the Harrisons inherited the property it contained a substantial quantity of table linen bearing the arms of Oliver Cromwell, a fine portrait of whom, in armour, hung over the chimney-piece in the sitting room. There was also a large brass medal embossed with the figure of the Protector mounted on horseback which, it was supposed, had once been worn by a soldier of the Common-wealth. These were significant discoveries in the light of our knowledge that John III supported the Parliamentary cause and did in fact marry the daughter of a senior officer in Cromwell's army.

By 1908 the house had been repaired and was reported at that time to be in 'perfectly good condition'. The tenants of Bishop Harrison were then a Mr. and Mrs. Caldwell who opened the door one day to find on their doorstep Mr. and Mrs. John Eldred of Sprouston, Boston, U.S.A. Mr. Eldred claimed descent from the Eldreds of Olivers.

Today the Olivers estate has shrunk to a mere 20 acres. Part of the original land is now a fruit farm, but the grounds surrounding the house have been well cared for. From the terrace on its south side one can look across formal gardens, ornamental lakes and a belt of woodland where, in the spring, choice varieties of rhododendrons and azaleas provide bursts of vivid colour among the trees. There is an ancient dove-cote in a nearby field, probably pre-dating the Eldreds, and close to the entrance of the drive, screened by trees, there is Little Olivers, a small, attractive 16th-century house where the steward or bailiff of the estate may once have lived. The ambience at Olivers remains wholly rural and enchanting. Long may it remain so!

Inside, the downstairs rooms are lofty and well-proportioned, with panelling in the reception hall, library, drawing and dining rooms. There is a recess in the hall which Bishop Harrison, on those occasions when he was living at Olivers, used as his private chapel. There are five bedrooms upstairs and four bathrooms, as well as attic rooms which could be converted into additional bedrooms. The house is centrally heated and there is garaging for five cars. The interior of the house, especially the first floor, has undergone extensive alterations and restoration in recent years, to the detriment of its period character. A sad loss was a rare crown-post truss that was removed from the dining room.

Much of the restoration was undertaken by a previous owner, David Papillon, a Colchester solicitor and one of the town's leading citizens. He was a bachelor and belonged to an old established Essex family. During his ownership of Olivers he must have spent a small fortune on the house and gardens. When he died a few years ago he left the house to Miles Park, architect and planning consultant of London, who sold it to the present owners, David and Gay Edwards. Mr. Park retained some of the land, on which he proposes to convert two barns into private residences and to name one of them 'Eldreds'.

Olivers has been the home of many lawyers during its long history. David Edwards is another and practises as a solicitor in London, to which he commutes every day from Colchester. His family is of school age and so, for the first time in many years, Olivers resounds with the lively noise of young people.

Until the Harrisons sold Olivers, the house contained a collection of family portraits which has now been dispersed. In 1802 Mr. Craven Ord, a fellow of the Archaeological Society of London, exhibited to the Society three 'curious old paintings' from this collection. The first showed a globe and bore the inscription:

> Thomas Eldred went out of Plymouth in 1586, and sailed round the whole globe, and arrived again in Plymouth on 9th September 1588. What can seem great to him, that hath seen the whole world and the wondrous works therein, save the Maker of it and the World above it?

The second picture was of an old man with a ruff, a short beard and whiskers, presumably Thomas Eldred himself, in commemoration of whom the Arms granted to his son, John I of Olivers, contain three globes and has for the crest a merman or triton. The third picture was of the ship in which Thomas made his epic voyage, or so Craven Ord supposed, for on the mainmast she was flying the Royal Arms, on the foremast the Cross of St George, on the third mast the Arms of the City of London, and on the fourth mast at the stern the Arms of Cavendish.

On the occasion of Mr. Steinman's visit to Olivers in 1837, he reported having seen nine other portraits of the Eldred family. They were all painted ovals of the schools of Kneller and Dahl, and were eventually given by Bishop Harrison to Sir Edward Ruggles-Brise, father of the present baronet, who, not having wall space on which to hang them, stored them in an attic room at his home in Spains Hall. There they languished until discovered by the present Sir John Ruggles-Brise and sold by him at Sothebys in January 1976. The pictures were offered in five lots and sold for £545.

The purchaser in each case was an art dealer, and most of the paintings are in the possession of collectors in the U.S.A. The exception is the portrait of Mary Eldred (neé Horsman), wife of John IV, which was found in a dealer's shop in Notting Hill in London two years after the sale. By a happy coincidence, John IV's portrait escaped the sale and was still hanging in the dining room at Spains Hall, Finchingfield. A private sale was arranged, and John IV's portrait has now joined that of his wife in the home, in England, of the author of this chapter. These two portraits are now the only identifiable mementoes surviving in England from the house of Olivers and of the Eldreds who once lived there.

Chapter Nine

Eldreds at the Court of St James

These are to require you to swear and admit John Eldred Esquire into the place and quality of Gentleman of His Majesty's Most Honourable Privy Chamber in Ordinary. To have, hold and exercise and enjoy the said place, together with all rights, profits, privileges and advantages therunto belonging in as full and ample a manner as any Gentleman of the Privy Chamber to his Majesty now holds, or of right ought to hold and enjoy the same. Given this fourth day of September, 1727, in the first year of his Majesty's reign.

Thus, on the authority of the Lord Chamberlain, was John Eldred of Great Saxham (1691-1746), the last of his line to live at Nutmeg Hall, appointed a Gentleman Usher of the Privy Chamber of King George II. He was also the first of two members of the family to serve the Royal Household. Both were descended from John Eldred, the famous merchant adventurer of the City of London and Great Saxham, and both bore the name 'John Eldred'. The second was an elder brother of Dodson Eldred whose son, Edward Jarvis Eldred, founded the family colony of Eldredville in Pennsylvania. This John Eldred was born in 1718 and was a Page to the Presence in the service of both George II and George III, as well as serving as Deputy Sergeant at Arms to the Prince Regent. He was by all accounts a remarkable man and lived until he was almost 100 years old.

But first let us consider the case of his cousin, John Eldred, who was a Gentleman of the Privy Chamber from 1727, when he was 36, until his death in 1746. Such appointments were eagerly sought by men of rank and influence, which undoubtedly John Eldred was. The office was a sinecure and the holder had few actual duties to perform. When it was created in the reign of Edward IV there was a salary attached to it, but all 'salaries, perquisites and fees' were abolished by James I, probably because he increased the number from 18 to 48. Aside from the prestige such appointments conferred upon their holders, there was usually exemption from jury service and from service in other public offices in the county, city or town, including that of sheriff (an office making heavy demands on the holder's pocket) except when there was no one else suitable for the job. In John Eldred's case, this caveat seemingly applied as he was High Sheriff of Suffolk in 1733-34.

Now let us go back to the other John Eldred who served the Court in the less exalted position of Page to the Presence, 'into the place and quality of which he was sworn and admitted' on 14 January 1754, eight years after the death of his kinsman. Such appointments, like those of the Gentleman of the Privy Chamber, were under the jurisdiction of the Lord Chamberlain who normally followed the custom of promoting a junior page or senior footman, although often, according to a writer on Court etiquette, 'the exercise of his Lordship's patronage was invoked by a higher power in favor of other candidates, which power was always obeyed'. Whether any strings were pulled in John Eldred's favour we shall never know, but the fact remains that a vacancy occurred for a Page to the Presence following the death of William Moseley, and John Eldred got the job.

The duties of the Page to the Presence (one at a time being in attendance) were to attend upon the Lords, Ladies and Maids of Honor in waiting at breakfast and luncheon, to be in communication with the Pages of the Back Stairs, and to wait upon the Monarch's visitors. In return for these services, John Eldred was entitled to enjoy, in the formal terms of his contract, 'all rights, profits, privileges and advantages of the post in as full and ample a manner as the said Mr. William Moseley formerly held'. What his rights, profits and privileges amounted to is uncertain, although we do know that 100 years later, in the reign of Queen Victoria, the salary of a Page to the Presence started at £140 a year and rose to £280 a year. The pages alternated between a month on duty and a month off. When on duty, they dined in the Steward's Room; when off duty, they received lodging money and board wages. In John Eldred's time they also received a quarterly cash allowance of £22 6s. 2d. in lieu of wax candles.

John was evidently a well-liked and respected figure in St James' Palace. He was considered to be good at his job, 'being very attentive to his duty'. Certainly John had an abundance of good spirits which, we are told, lasted throughout his life. He had something to say to everybody and liked to boast about his favourite habits of eating and drinking. His particular choice of beverage was porter and, according to his obituary in the *Gentleman's Magazine*, he would often consume as much as three quarts a day. From the same source, we learn that he occasionally took a glass of British gin and water and that he smoked incessantly. In addition, he would put away a pound of rump steak at a sitting – a practice he followed until within a fortnight of his death.

That John Eldred's remarkable constitution did not weaken in old age is proven by the fact that he must have been aged at least 90 when he carried one of the heavy maces before the Prince Regent as Deputy Sergeant at Arms when the Prince went in state to the Chapel Royal. He ascribed his good health to the regular weekly exercise which he had taken for some 50 years. This consisted of walking from his apartment in the Lord Steward's Court in St James' Palace to the Tothill Fields area of Westminster where he collected rents on some of his property. Twice a widower, he did his own shopping at the same time and would go to several butchers' shops before he found a rump of beef from which a steak could be cut that would please him. He would take this and other provisions home for his servant to cook.

In 1805, according to the Royal Archives in Windsor Castle, John Eldred retired from his duties as Page to the Presence; 'An exceedingly obliging man', is how a friend of his summed him up, 'and accommodating to every person who had the pleasure of knowing him'.

Chapter Ten

The Tragedy of Anne Hutchinson (1591-1643)

Lieutenant Thomas[2] Eldred (1648-1726), son of Samuel[1] and Elizabeth (Miller) Eldred, married Susanna Cole, daughter of John and Susanna (Hutchinson) Cole. Susanna Hutchinson was the daughter of William and Anne (Marbury) Hutchinson. Anne Hutchinson voiced the principle of free speech, assembly and religion; the story of this remarkable woman is a memorable one.

On the eastern border of Lincolnshire lies Alford, a market town of considerable antiquity. Its site, a plain with a background of wooded hills, is on the northern side of the fens memorable as the scene of the last stand of the Saxons against William the Conqueror. Alford may be considered a historic centre, for its neighbourhood has witnessed events that have left their impress on the world's history. A semi-circle, with a radius of some 60 miles, drawn west of Alford, will include Scrooby, Bawtry and Austerfield, whence went forth Bradford, Brewster and their fellow Pilgrims to learn in Holland the lessons which enabled them to found a new state in a New World; Epworth, the birthplace of John Wesley, founder of Methodism; Boston – Saint Botolph's town – parent of Boston of the New World; Huntingdon, the home of Oliver Cromwell; and Groton, the birthplace of John Winthrop, founder of Massachusetts. Two miles south of Alford is the hamlet of Willoughby, the birthplace of Captain John Smith, founder of Virginia, while Alford itself was the home of Anne Hutchinson.

Alford is on the border of a highly cultivated agricultural district, but the town itself is much the same as it was four centuries ago, its houses clustered on a single street a third of a mile long, watered by a rivulet. In the 16th century Alford possessed some 230 houses with a population of a little more than 1,000 souls.

At the close of the 16th and beginning of the 17th century, among the prominent families in or near Alford were the Hutchinsons and the Marburys. The Hutchinsons were earlier of Lincoln, where several of the name had achieved eminence. John Hutchinson, born in 1515, was successively High Sheriff of Lincolnshire and Alderman and Mayor of Lincoln. He died in 1565 while serving a second term as mayor. His eldest son succeeded to many of his honours, but his youngest son, Edward, born in 1564, moved to Alford and resided there until his death in 1632. Edward Hutchinson left 11 children, the eldest of whom, William, baptized on 14 August 1586, became the husband of his more famous wife, Anne Hutchinson.

The Marburys were connected with some of the best blood in the kingdom. Francis Marbury, the father of Anne Hutchinson, was the third son of William Marbury, Esq., of Girsby, Lincolnshire, and of Agnes, daughter of John Lenton, Esq. He married, first, Elizabeth Moore, by whom he had three daughters. His second wife was Bridget, daughter of John Dryden, Esq., of Canons Ashby, Northamptonshire, by his wife Elizabeth, daughter of Sir John Cope, Knight. By this second marriage Francis Marbury had 11 more children, and Anne, the second child, was baptized at Alford on 20 July 1591. Her mother's eldest brother, Erasmus Dryden, created a baronet in 1619, was the grandfather of the poet laureate John Dryden. Anne Hutchinson was, therefore, second cousin to John Dryden.

Francis Marbury is always mentioned in the parish records at Alford with the affix 'Gentleman'. He must have entered into holy orders, for in 1605 he was Rector of St Martin's Vintry, London. In 1607-8 he was presented to St Pancras, Soper Lane, which charge he resigned two years later on his presentation to St Margaret's in New Fish Street. This last parish he held, in conjunction with St Martin's Vintry, until his death in 1610-11.

William Hutchinson and Anne Marbury were married on 9 August 1612 in the church of St Mary Woolnoth, Lombard Street, London. They returned to Alford and made that place their home, and in its parish registers are recorded the baptisms of 14 children born to them between 1613 and 1633, the year before their departure to the New World.

The precise reasons for the family leaving their native land are not known; it was probably because of the religious, political and social unrest which was sweeping over England. Puritanism had divided the Church of England and brought into being a new political party. Archbishop Laud, foremost in Church and State, was eager in the persecution of those who differed from him, and the king, ruling without a parliament, was harassing the people for ship-money. Freedom of speech was interdicted. Whoever held opinions antagonistic to those in power was obliged to renounce political honours and emoluments, and was denied social advancement. To remain in England was to subject oneself and one's children to persecution, and many principal families, able to leave, sought retreats where they were free to practise their religion in peace. Some fled to Germany, some to Holland, and very many to the New World. Within a score of years after the landing of the Pilgrims in 1620, more than 20,000 emigrants sought new homes in New England alone.

Another, and perhaps stronger, reason for the emigration of the Hutchinsons was the departure in 1633 of the Rev. John Cotton from Boston, where he had officiated for 20 years as vicar of St Botolph's. His inclination towards Puritanism had attracted the attention of Archbishop Laud, and to escape imprisonment Cotton had to flee. He sailed in the *Griffin* for New England, landing in Boston in September 1636. The Hutchinsons and the Cottons had been friends for a long time. Mrs. Hutchinson had sat under Cotton's ministrations for so long that she had become thoroughly imbued with his teaching. His departure for the New World must have influenced the Hutchinsons in their decision to emigrate, and it is probable that they would have accompanied him but for the birth of their last child, Susanna, which occurred in November 1633, shortly after Cotton's departure. The fact that Cotton's wife was pregnant did not delay his departure, and a son was born to them on the passage. He was named, in consequence, Seaborn. In anticipation of their own emigration, the Hutchinsons entrusted their eldest son, Edward, then 20 years old, to Mr. Cotton's care, and he accompanied him in the *Griffin*. With Edward was his uncle, Edward Hutchinson, the youngest brother of William, and his wife, who both returned to England after 1638. The elder Edward Hutchinson became a freeman in Boston on

4 March, and the younger Edward followed on 3 September 1634, both before the arrival of William's family. In the following year, 1634, William and Anne Hutchinson sailed for New England in the same ship, the *Griffin*, with 10 children, three others having been buried at Alford. William was then 48 and his wife 43 years old. Accompanying them was William's aged mother, Mrs. Susanna Hutchinson (his father had died two years previously), his brother Samuel and his sister Mary, wife of the Rev. John Wheelwright, afterwards prominent in the Antinomian controversy.

The Hutchinsons landed in Boston on 18 September 1634 and two months later the father of the family was admitted to the Boston church, and the wife and four eldest children were made members shortly afterwards. In March 1635 William Hutchinson and his sons, Richard and Francis, became freemen of the colony, and in the following May William was chosen to represent Boston in the General Court.

William Hutchinson's house in Boston stood on the corner of Washington and School Streets, on the site of the since famous Old Corner Bookstore. Almost opposite was the residence of Governor Winthrop. Mrs. Hutchinson took a prominent place in the Church almost from the time of her admission, asserting herself and her views as much as she could. She was foremost, too, in works of mercy and charity, and soon became the most prominent woman in the colony.

Before Mrs. Hutchinson's arrival, the women of Boston had meekly borne the indignity of not speaking in church, but she was of different stuff. She had well-settled opinions concerning the great questions which then agitated men's minds and she saw no reason why she should be curbed in expressing those opinions. For the purpose of airing her views, she invited the women to meet at her house for discussions similar to those which weekly drew together the men of the congregation. The experiment proved a success, and the assemblies often numbered 60 to 80 persons. At first the ministers and elders favoured these meetings and smiled upon Mrs. Hutchinson's efforts. Mr. Cotton writes that she was 'well-beloved, and all the faithful embraced her conference and blessed God for her fruitful discourses'. Her meetings were looked upon as a spiritual awakening and all believed that through them souls might be brought to Christ. Presently some of the ministers made the discovery that Mrs. Hutchinson had ideas not always in consonance with their teachings, however, so they began to look askance at these gatherings, which had attained such popularity that they were held twice a week. In time they conspired to put an end to them.

To understand the situation thoroughly, we must glance briefly at the Constitution of the Massachusetts Colony and at the politico-religious policy of those who controlled it. The Puritans who left England 10 years later than the Pilgrim Fathers were not, as they were, Separatists, but claimed still to retain connections with the Mother Church. They were simply Non-Conformists, refusing to conform to the Church ceremonial because it tended to lessen the chasm between Protestantism and Roman Catholicism. As those who advocated these ideas suffered persecution, they determined to seek a new land where they could build up a Church and society in accord with their views. But no sooner had they established themselves in the New World than they became even more intolerant than those from whose persecutions they had fled. They left Old England ostensibly for the sake of religious liberty; they established in New England an oligarchy where even the suggestion of religious liberty was treason.

As early as 1631 it was enacted that no one but a church member should be made a freeman, and no one could become a church member unless proposed with the consent of the minister of the congregation. Thus the ministers controlled not only the church but the body politic. The Bay Colony (Massachusetts) was a theocracy, in which every power was subordinated to an oligarchy of theologians.

The Hutchinson family had been in Boston for about a year when Mr. Roger Williams (Rhode Island) was banished, but, though Mrs. Hutchinson must have been conversant with his opinions, there is nothing to show that she took any part in the famous controversy. Yet there can be little doubt, from the character of her teachings, that she was permeated with his ideas in regard to soul liberty and that she was as far advanced in opinion as he was. By one Puritan authority she is spoken of as 'like Roger Williams, or worse'.

In October 1635, the very month when sentence of banishment was passed against Mr. Williams, Mr. Henry Vane landed in Boston. Winthrop, later inimical to him, was at first his friend. He writes:

> One Mr. Henry Vane, son and heir to Sir Henry Vane, comptroller of the King's house, who, being a young gentleman of excellent parts, and had been employed by his father (when he was Ambassador) in foreign affairs; yet, being called to the obedience of the gospel, forsook the honours and preferments of the court, to enjoy the ordinances of Christ in their purity here.

Mr. Vane was admitted almost immediately to the Boston church, and at the next election, in the following March, was chosen as Governor to succeed Mr. Haynes. At this time Mrs. Hutchinson, who had been a member of the Boston church for over a year, had developed, through her lectures and personal influence, a very strong following. Among her friends was the Rev. Mr. Cotton, the colleague of Mr. Wilson, and Governor Vane soon enrolled himself amongst her staunchest supporters, but unfortunately for her, Mr. Winthrop held aloof:

> One Mrs. Hutchinson, a member of the church in Boston, a woman of a ready wit and bold spirit, brought over with her two dangerous errors: (1) That the person of the Holy Ghost dwells in a justified person. (2) That no sanctification can help to evidence to us our justification. From these two grew many branches, as (1) Our Union with the Holy Ghost, so as a Christian remains dead in every spiritual action, and hath no gifts nor graces, other than such as are in hypocrites, nor any other sanctifications but the Holy Ghost himself. There joined with her in these opinions a brother of hers, one Mr. Wheelwright, a silenced minister sometimes in England.

This slighting reference to the Rev. John Wheelwright, one of the most distinguished clergymen of his day, 'whose long life', says the Hon. James Savage, 'afforded him a triumph over the injustice of intolerance', is characteristic of Winthrop's narrow-mindedness. Mr. Wheelwright was not Mrs. Hutchinson's brother, but the brother-in-law of her husband, through marriage with William Hutchinson's sister

Mary. He was a graduate of Cambridge and had been for some years a clergyman of the established church until dispossessed by Archbishop Laud. He came to Boston in 1636 and was chosen pastor of a branch church in what is now Braintree. Because his opinions differed from those of Mr. Wilson, the pastor of Boston, and his associates, he suffered contumely, persecution and banishment; but more fortunate than some of the other sufferers in that strange episode of Massachusett's history, he was finally permitted to return and lived long enough to see the triumph of many of the principles he had advocated and for which he had suffered.

The principal points of Mrs. Hutchinson's teachings are set out by Mr. Winthrop. She probably taught that the Holy Ghost dwelt in the person of the believer, but the deductions drawn by Winthrop were largely his own and were not admitted by Mrs. Hutchinson. She also maintained the doctrine of justification by faith as opposed to justification by works; and, as her opponents asserted, claimed to be 'under a covenant of works'. The Rev. John Cotton was largely responsible for her opinions. Cotton, of a sanguine temperament and strong emotional nature, was given to softening the rigidity of the teachings of Puritanism by preaching the happiness of the elect and the joys awaiting the true believer.

Mrs. Hutchinson, Cotton's ardent disciple in both old and new Boston, followed closely in his footsteps and emphasised in her meetings his favourite doctrines. Support for her views came from most members of the Boston church, only five dissenting from her, but among those five were Winthrop, who had grown jealous of Governor Vane, and Mr. Wilson, who was envious of the popularity of Mr. Cotton, and who saw in Mrs. Hutchinson's conferences a usurpation of ministerial functions.

The controversy growing out of the discussion of these two points of doctrine divided the church and, if we are to believe Mrs. Hutchinson's enemies, came near to disrupting the State. The colony separated into two hostile factions, those supporting the views of Mrs. Hutchinson under the leadership of Governor Vane, and her opponents under that of Mr. Winthrop.

The quarrel became so bitter that Mrs. Hutchinson's opponents, resenting her characterisation of them as living under a covenant of works, sought the records of past heresies to find terms of opprobrium to apply to her and her followers. At first they called them Opportunists and Familists, and finally Antinomians, as being *anti nomos*, against the (moral) law. This was probably suggested by a comparison of her teachings with those of John Agricola, chaplain of the Elector of Saxony in 1526, who carried to an extreme Luther's doctrine of justification by faith as opposed to good works. Agricola maintained that the moral law was superseded by the gospel, that it is not binding on Christians, and that a child of God cannot sin. The Massachusetts authorities, who held this to be a grossly immoral doctrine, saddled the heresy on Mrs. Hutchinson. Some went even further and stooped to personal abuse. Mrs. Hutchinson was connected with the licentious sect of Familists or members of the Family of Love in Holland. Mr. Cotton believed, with Mrs. Hutchinson, in salvation by grace.

28. Memorial to Anne Hutchinson.

In March 1637 the Rev. Mr. Wheelwright, who had become one of Mrs. Hutchinson's most ardent supporters, preached a sermon on a fast day in which he asserted that 'those under a covenant of grace must prepare for battle and come out and fight with spiritual weapons against pagans, and anti-Christians, and those that runne under a covenant of works'. For this utterance, claimed to be seditious, he was called before the General Court and notwithstanding the protestation of Governor Vane, who condemned the proceedings of the court, he was censured. A petition justifying the sermon and the preacher was signed by nearly all the members of the Boston church, but the Court took no notice of it. Some of the friends of Mr. Wheelwright then threatened an appeal to England. This only added fuel to the flames, for in the colony 'it was accounted perjury and treason to speak of appeals to the King'.

So virulent had the controversy grown that the opponents of Mrs. Hutchinson, consisting chiefly of members of churches outside Boston, determined that the next General Court of election should be held in Newtown (now Cambridge), beyond her influence. At this court, marked by tumultuous proceedings and fierce speeches, some of the brethren going so far as to lay violent hands on each other, Governor Vane was defeated and Winthrop was elected in his place. Events now proceeded rapidly. The political horizon being thus cleared, it was adjudged a fitting time to purge the colony of heresy and to prescribe what was and what was not proper for the churches to believe. Therefore a synod of all the teaching elders throughout the country was called to meet at Newtown. Ministers gathered from near and far, even Hartford and the other towns in the Connecticut Valley (then under the jurisdiction of Massachusetts) sending their delegates. For more than three weeks this assembly wrestled with points of doctrine, erroneous opinions and unwholesome expressions, and after much wrangling and many heated debates, during which the Governor had frequently to interpose and sometimes even to adjourn to give the contestants time to cool off, a long list of errors, 82 in all, were condemned.

Governor Vane, in disgust at the turn of affairs, had meantime returned to England, but others of the Boston church took offence at the production of such an array of errors, asserting that it was a causeless reproach upon the country, and calling for the names of the persons who held these errors. The majority replied vaguely that all these opinions could be proved to be held by some in the country, but declined 'to name the parties because the assembly had not to do with persons, but doctrines only'. Mr. Cotton, who had been forced by the weight of opinion against him to modify his views, gave a qualified assent to the conclusions, but withheld his signature. He contented himself with saying that he 'disrelished all those opinions and expressions as being some of them heretical, some of them blasphemous, some of them erroneous, and all of them incongruous'. Ten years later he wrote concerning the synod: 'Such as endeavored the healing of these distempers did seem to me to be transported with more jealousies, and heats, and paroxyms of spirit then would well stand with brotherly love, or the rule of the gospel'.

The heresies being thus extirpated, the coast was clear to proceed against the heretics. Mr. Wheelwright was disenfranchised and banished from the colony, and those who had signed or taken part in the petition on his behalf were either banished or otherwise punished. The Court then summoned Mrs. Hutchinson and charged her, says Winthrop:

with divers matters, as her keeping two public lectures in her house, whereat sixty or eighty persons did usually resort, and for reproaching most of the ministers, (viz., all except Mr. Cotton) for not preaching a covenant of free grace, and that they had not the seal of the spirit, nor were able ministers of the New Testament; which were clearly proved against her, though she sought to shift it off.

The first of these charges, that she kept 'two public lectures in her house' seems trivial enough to the present generation, but it was among the heresies condemned by the synod. One of the resolutions passed by the assembled clerical wisdom, as quoted by Winthrop, reads:

> That though women might meet (some few together) to pray and edify one another; yet such an assembly (as was then in practice in Boston), where sixty or more did meet every week, and one woman (in a prophetical way, by resolving questions of doctrine, and expounding Scripture) took upon her the whole exercise, was agreed to be disorderly without rule.

Mr. Cotton made a feeble attempt to defend her, but his own position was not secure enough to permit him to espouse her cause too openly. Others who spoke on her behalf were brow-beaten. Winthrop, who knew her best, acted as chief inquisitor. It is difficult to conceive, in these days of toleration, of the standards of justice of our forefathers. This woman was brought before a court of prejudiced men, in which her accusers were her judges, was allowed no counsel nor permitted to call witnesses, and was subjected to hours of interrogation by the best intellect of the day. She was forced to stand during her trial, which lasted two days, until she almost fell from exhaustion, yet no word of complaint appears to have fallen from her lips. Though the court was called to convict, so little was proved against her and so bewildered were her judges by Cotton's ambiguous and sophistical arguments that she would probably have been acquitted but for her own undaunted truthfulness. She disdained to refute any of the accusations, and even went to the extent of denying the authority of her judges, declaring that they would suffer disaster for her persecution. 'So', says Winthrop, 'the court proceeded and banished her; but because it was winter, they committed her to a private house, where she was well provided, and her own friends and the elders permitted to go to her, but none else'.

Winthrop is somewhat disingenuous in this. The private house to which the prisoner was assigned was not in Boston, as one would judge from the context, but in Roxbury, where she was far from her husband, children, and friends. She was committed to the custody of Mr. Joseph Welde, brother of her bitter enemy, the minister of Roxbury. 'To be committed to prison in another town', says Mr. Savage, 'even at the house of so good a man as Mr. Welde, might not be an agreeable process of conversion; but when subjected to the perpetual buzzing of the clerical tormentor, she must have been more than woman, not to prove incorrigible'. The authorities now turned their attention to her followers. As these consisted of the best men of Boston and the surrounding towns, they did not dare to accuse them openly of treason; so they trumped up against them a cause of suspicion, asserting a fear that they were about to rise in armed rebellion, and ordered them to surrender their arms and ammunition.

As religious intolerance had led to the severance of Roger Williams from Massachusetts and had been a considerable factor in determining the emigration of Mr. Hooker and his friends to the Connecticut Valley, so the dissensions which had grown out of the Hutchinson controversy led the friends of that gentlewoman to meditate another secession, with the project of a new settlement on Long Island or Delaware Bay. To the student of history it will be interesting to glance briefly at the names of some of the adherents of this persecuted woman who were willing to follow her into exile. At their head were Dr. John Clarke, a learned physician, and William Coddington, Treasurer of the Colony and reputedly the wealthiest man in Boston. The latter was afterwards for many years Governor of Rhode Island, the former Deputy Governor and long the colony's trusted agent in London. Among the others were William Hutchinson, who succeeded Coddington as Judge (that is, Governor) in the first settlement on Rhode Island; his son Edward, ancestor of the last Royal Governor of Massachusetts; John Sanford, later Governor of Rhode Island; John Coggeshall, first President of Rhode Island under the patent; Thomas Savage, later Commander-in-Chief of the Massachusetts forces at the beginning of King Philip's war; William Aspinwall, Assistant Secretary of Rhode Island; William Dyer, Secretary and Attorney General of Rhode Island; Henry Bull, Deputy, Assistant and Governor; and representatives of many (Robinson) families prominent. What was Massachusetts' loss was Rhode Island's gain. The high character of the men thus driven into the wilderness gave an impetus to the small beginnings already made by Roger Williams and his friends at Providence, and helped to build up the first state in the history of the world founded on principles now recognized as fundamental.

The disenfranchised and banished partisans of Mrs. Hutchinson shook the dust of Boston from their feet and journeyed southward looking for a new home. Roger Williams persuaded them to settle in his neighbourhood and, through his influence with the natives, the island of Aquidneck in Narragansett Bay (later named Rhode Island), was bought and a settlement made at Pocasset (or Portsmouth) on the northernmost end. The colony increased so rapidly that in the following spring a portion separated and founded a new township at the southern end of the island which was named New Port, now Newport, the summer metropolis of America.

Meanwhile, Mrs. Hutchinson was removed to Mr. Cotton's house in Boston, in order that the latter and other ministers might have the opportunity to convert her, if possible, from the error of her ways; but, to the astonishment of the good men who reasoned with her, she declined to have her religious ideas run into the cast-iron mould prescribed by them as the only way of attaining heavenly joy. 'After much time and many arguments had been spent to bring her to see her sin, but all in vain', says Winthrop, 'the church with one consent, cast her out'. He adds: 'After she was excommunicated, her spirits, which seemed before to be somewhat dejected, revived again, and she gloried in her sufferings, saying that it was the greatest happiness, next to Christ, that ever befell her'.

Two or three days later Governor Winthrop 'sent a warrant to Mrs. Hutchinson to depart this jurisdiction before the last of this month'. She left Boston on one of the last days of March 1638, going by boat to Mount Wollaston (Braintree), where her husband had a farm. Thence she went by land to Providence and soon after joined her husband and family on Rhode Island.

Anne Hutchinson's active life ended with her banishment. In her new home, where she was surrounded by men and women in accord with her own sentiments, she might have passed the rest of her days in contentment and peace had not the jealousy and hatred of her enemies in Massachusetts followed her even there. Winthrop, whose bitter nature was often overshadowed in dealing with opponents by narrow prejudices and superstition, seized every opportunity to cast slurs on her. He records in his history every vague report concerning her that reaches his ears, in one case going beyond the bounds of decency to give the disgusting details of a matter which he says was openly discussed in a lecture in Boston. It is now almost impossible to read appreciatively the records of trivial circumstances, treated by our forefather as vital to religion and morality, which seems in the light of the present worthy only of pity and contempt. While all must recognise the nobler elements of Mr. Winthrop's character and give him credit for honesty and sincerity, we cannot pass in silence the narrowness which characterised him.

So acrimonious grew the relations between the elect in Boston and the miserable sinners whom they had cast out that the people of Rhode Island were forbidden to come into the jurisdiction of Massachusetts under pain of death. Even Roger Williams did not dare to go to Boston to take ship for England when sent thither on the colony's business, but was obliged to go to New Amsterdam to seek passage of a Dutch vessel. In 1641 Mrs. Hutchinson's son, Francis, and her son-in-law had occasion to go to Boston. As soon as their presence was known they were ordered before the Governor and Council. As they did not acknowledge the jurisdiction of Massachusetts, they refused. The constable, therefore, brought them into court, where Mr. Collins was charged with having written a letter declaring, says Winthrop, 'all our churches and ministers to be anti-Christian, and many other reproachful speeches'. Mr. Collins acknowledged the letter and maintained it, but also 'maintained that there were no Gentile churches (as he termed them) since the Apostles' times, and that none could ordain ministers, etc. Francis Hutchinson did agree with him in some of these but not resolutely in all'. This, however, was enough, and they were committed to prison. Mr. Collins was fined £100 and Francis Hutchinson £50, and the court ordered them to be kept in prison until they gave security. Winthrop commented:

> We assessed the fines the higher partly that by occasion thereof they might be the longer kept in from doing harm (for they were kept close prisoners) and also because that family had put the country to so much charge in the synod and other occasions to the value of £500 at least; but after, because the winter drew on, and the prison was inconvenient, we abated them to £40 and £20. But they seemed not willing to pay anything. They refused to come to the church assemblies except they were led, and so they came duly. At last we took their own bonds for their fine, and so dismissed them.

The only comment necessary on this narrative is that Francis Hutchinson, who thus sinned against the ordinances of Massachusetts, was then just 20 years old and his companion little older. In the next year, 1642, William Hutchinson, the father, died in Newport. The settlement on Rhode Island was then but four years old, and there was still some doubt about the permanency of the new colony. Plymouth claimed that some of its territory was within her bounds, and Massachusetts laid covetous eyes on its fertile lands and magnificent bay. Providence and Rhode Island gave shelter to those who had left Massachusetts for conscience sake or who had been expelled for offences against her laws. There, free from her vengeance, they scoffed at her ordinances and defied her power. This was, of course, very irritating. In the belief that they would be doing God's will in driving these disaffected spirits further into the wilderness, the authorities of the Bay Colony set on foot a movement to extend their jurisdiction over the Narragansett country. The mere apprehension of the possible success of such a movement caused consternation in Rhode Island and led some inhabitants to look for homes further away from the vengeance of Massachusetts. Among these was Mrs. Hutchinson who, now without the protection of a husband, derived from these rumours the belief that Newport was no longer a safe refuge for her family. The country west of Narragansett was controlled partly by Massachusetts and partly by Connecticut, whose chief minister, Mr. Davenport, had taken part in the proceedings against her, so she saw no safety short of the Dutch settlements beyond New Haven. Several English families had already settled in that region, notably Captain John Underhill at Greenwich and the Throgmortons and Cornells nearer New Amsterdam. Mrs. Hutchinson removed to her new home probably in the autumn of 1642. She bought property on what is now Pelham Neck and built a house near a tributary of the river now called Hutchinson's River. This was long called Black Dog Brook, possibly from some connection with Mrs. Hutchinson's fate, and, later, Hutchinson Brook. The site of her home, the remains of the foundations of which were visible within the past generation, was near a large boulder called Split Rock, through which a tree grows. It is now included in Pelham Bay Park, Borough of the Bronx, within the limits of New York City.

Mrs. Hutchinson was unfortunate in selecting this time for a removal. The Dutch Governor, Kieft, had aroused the enmity of the savages by his inhumanity and treachery, and red men, provoked to fury, resolved to exterminate the Dutch and all connected with them. They ravaged the Long Island, plundering and burning, and swept Manhattan Island to the gate of the fort at New Amsterdam. It is possible that Mrs. Hutchinson, whose knowledge of native American character had been gained by intercourse with the gentler Narragansetts, propitiated and made friendly by Roger Williams and his associates, may have considered herself safe in her exposed situation. However, the savages of her new home were very different from those she had met in Rhode Island. They were known as the Siwanoys, a clan of the Mohegan tribe.

We know little of the final catastrophe beyond that it happened in August 1643. The savages that drove the Dutch to seek shelter within the walls of Fort Amsterdam burned her house and slew every person save one, the youngest daughter Susanna, a child of nine years, who was carried into captivity. Most historians of this event say that Mrs. Hutchinson and all her family were cut down, but this is far from the truth. Of the children brought to the New World, five at least married and left families.

IN MEMORY OF
ANNE MARBURY HUTCHINSON
BAPTIZED AT ALFORD
LINCOLNSHIRE · ENGLAND
20 · JULY · 1591
KILLED BY THE INDIANS
AT EAST CHESTER NEW YORK 1643
A COURAGEOUS EXPONENT
OF CIVIL LIBERTY
AND RELIGIOUS TOLERATION

29. Detail of the memorial to Anne Hutchinson.

Mrs. Hutchinson was accompanied in her last migration only by her son Francis, then a young man of 22 years, her son-in-law the Rev. Mr. Collins, and his wife, her daughter Anne, and four other children. If, as some record, 16 persons in all were killed, the remainder were either servants or members of other families slain in the same massacre. It is interesting to note that the neck where the tragedy occurred, a little east of Throg's Neck, was called Anne's Hoeck or Hook, in memory of the outcast of Boston, and the property including it was named the Manor of Anne Hoeck's Neck. The savage who claimed the honour of slaying Mrs. Hutchinson assumed her Christian name, and 11 years after the catastrophe, when he and others confirmed a deed of the property to Dr. Thomas Pell, he signed himself 'Ann Hoeck alias Wampage'. The property was next called 'Hutchinsons', and in 1664, when Thomas Pell granted to James Eustis, Phillip Pinckney and others the right to settle 'at Hutchinsons, that is where the house stood at the meadows', the place was named 'Ten Families', from the fact that that number settled there. Still later it was named after the Pell family, Pelham, the second element from the Anglo-Saxon signifying home or dwelling.

Susanna Hutchinson, the daughter carried away into captivity, remained with the savages for four years, almost long enough to become one of them. She was finally ransomed when 13 years old by the Dutch, and returned to her family in Boston, where she eventually married John Cole. Of the other children who survived, Captain Edward, the eldest son, was killed in the services of Massachusetts in King Philip's war in 1675. He was the father of Hon. Elisha Hutchinson, father of the Hon. Thomas, who in turn was father of the more famous Thomas, the celebrated historian and last Royal Governor of Massachusetts. From Elizabeth, daughter of Captain Edward, was descended the wife of John Singleton Copley, whose son became Lord Lyndhurst, Lord Chancellor of England. Another of Captain Edward's daughters, Susanna, married Nathaniel Coddington, son of Governor William Coddington and of Anne Brinley, daughter of Thomas Brinley, Auditor General of both Charles I and Charles II.

Of Anne Hutchinson's other daughters, Faith married Major Thomas Savage and became the ancestress of the noted historian and genealogist of New England, and Bridget became the wife of Governor John Sanford and the mother of another Governor of Rhode Island, Peleg Sanford.

It would be gratifying if we were able to record, in conclusion, that the sad fate of Mrs. Hutchinson and her children brought remorse into the hearts of those who were primarily resposible for it, but even the usually gentle Winthrop had only sarcasm for the catastrophe. He remarks, after detailing the facts of her death:

> These people cast off ordinances and churches, and now at last their own people, and for larger accommodations had subjected themselves to the Dutch and dwelt scatteringly near a mile or under; and some that escaped, who had removed only for want (as they said) of hay for their cattle which increased much, now coming back again, they wanted cattle for their grass.

George Bishop, the author of *New England Judged*, tells us that Winthrop repented of his harshness on his death-bed six years later. As the story goes, when Mr. Dudley, then Deputy Governor, pressed him to sign an order of banishment on a heterodox person, he refused, saying 'I have done much of that work already'. The Rev. Mr. Welde, who was in England at the time of the massacre, writes of it in a spirit of pious exultation: 'The Lord heard our groans to heaven, and freed us from our great and sore affliction'. He continues:

> Now I am come to the last act of her tragedy, a most heavy stroke upon herself and hers, as I received it very lately from a godly hand in New England ... The Indians set upon them, and slew her, and all her family, her daughter and her daughter's husband, and all their children, save one that escaped; (her own husband being dead before); a dreadful blow ... I have never heard that the Indians in those parts did ever before this commit the like outrage upon any one family or families, and therefore God's hand is the more apparently seen herein, to pick out this woeful woman, to make her, and those belonging to her, an unheard of heavy example of their cruelty above others.

Today, when nearly three centuries have passed, we, who are many of us descended from both parties in that memorable episode, can look back with philosophical equanimity at the questions that were considered important enough to divide churches and to threaten the existence of states, and judge with impartiality the actors who honestly took opposite sides in them. Massachusetts, yet in her infancy, was confronted with conflicting policies, the one involving religious toleration, the other compulsory theological conformity. She chose the latter, and it coloured her history and her institutions for more than a century and a half.

Mrs. Hutchinson turned the tide in the other direction, only to be overwhelmed by it, but was far in advance of her time. 'She was a woman', says Eggleston, 'cursed with a natural gift for leadership in an age that had no place for such women'. Having this gift she was unable to stifle her longings to give expression to it, and so, says Adam, she attempted a premature revolt against an organized and firmly rooted oligarchy of theocrats'. Failure was inevitable, for the time was not yet ripe; but, advanced as we are today, who can tell what our progress might not have been had religious tolerance and civil liberty – the ideas of Roger Williams, of Henry Vane, and of Anne Hutchinson – prevailed earlier throughout New England.

The ashes of Anne Hutchinson lie beneath the soil of Pelham Bay Park, New York City. In May 1911, a bronze tablet was placed by the Colonial Dames of the State of New York on Split Rock, near the site of Mrs. Hutchinson's home in 1643. It has been said that the 'cherry tree in the cleft of Split Rock was in full bloom at the time, as if nature sought to crown the event with her approval'.

Note: *This story was written originally by John Denison Champlin and published in the New York Times in 1904. This story was republished for private distribution by William Henry Eldridge in 1913.*

Chapter Eleven

Pocahontas, the Indian Princess (c.1595-1617)

Pocahontas was the daughter of the great Algonquin Chief Powhatan who ruled a vast area of land along the Atlantic seaboard. Her tribal name was Matoaka, which means 'little snow feather' or 'leaping stream among the hills' or 'little frolic'. Pocahontas could be called America's first folk heroine because she has been idealised and immortalised throughout the four centuries since she died. Some accounts of her deeds are so ridiculously sentimental or obviously exaggerated that they can only be regarded as legends or figments of various writers' imaginations. The most famous of her supposed deeds is, of course, the story of her rescue of Captain John Smith, one of the founders of Jamestown, the first English settlement in America, established in 1607. Although the first published account of this deed was in John Smith's book *True Relation of Virginia*, the tale has always been marred by controversy. The story does not stand up well under the scrutiny of 20th-century scholarly research. Yet, as it was first related in writing by a respected leader of the Jamestown settlement and since it is such a dramatically appealing and famous story, recounting the tale is justified.

Captain John Smith was an adventurer. He had voluntarily fought in several conflicts in Europe before joining the first group of Englishmen to sail to America for the purpose of founding a colony in the New World. But once there, instead of settling down to the hard labour of clearing land, planting crops, helping to build warm and secure shelters and so on, Smith preferred to roam up and down the coast exploring and making maps. It was on one of these trips that he was captured by the Indians and taken to their chief, Powhatan. The Algonquin chief decided that Smith should be put to death by having his brains bashed out. The Englishman was ordered to kneel and wedge his head between two large stones. Just as two warriors were about to smash his head with stone war clubs, Pocahontas, Powhatan's daughter, came to the Englishman's rescue. At the time, she was only about ten years old. As the little girl saw what was about to happen to her father's prisoner, she rushed forward, placed her head on top of his, and began to plead with her father to spare Smith's life. Powhatan could not deny his beloved daughter her wish and declared that Smith's life would be spared. As was customary among the Algonquins under such circumstances, John Smith was adopted into Powhatan's family and was shortly thereafter allowed to return to Jamestown. From this time on, Pocahontas often went into Jamestown, sometimes with Indians delivering food to the settlers. On those trips she often saw John Smith. He was kind and gracious to the young girl, taught her English words and phrases, and generally showed his gratitude to her.

This story raises a lot of questions regarding its authenticity, even though the first person to relate it in writing was John Smith himself, first in a letter to Queen Anne, consort to King James, in 1616 and then in his book of 1624. It is questionable that a doting father would permit his daughter to be present at such an execution. It is more likely that a 10-year-old girl would have fled from such a sight. If it was common for her to watch such executions, it is unlikely that she would have dashed forward to save a man who was a stranger to her, and a white man. Powhatan may have decided to spare Smith's life because, if he did so, Smith would according to Algonquin custom be adopted into Powhatan's family and would in turn be obliged to bring gifts to the chief, possibly guns. It is strange that Smith said nothing at all about his rescue by Pocahontas in the first edition of his book. It is also strange that Smith, who was later in London at the same time as Pocahontas, called on her only once, and that was in the seventh month of her stay. Unfortunately, there is no record of Pocahontas' version of this tale. It is the most famous of a number of stories about the Indian princess which can never be proven or disproven.

When she was about thirteen years old, Pocahontas married an Indian named Kocoum. They were married for no more than two years, and his fate is not known. Pocahontas was not seen in Jamestown during this period, and we know nothing of her life at this time.

By 1612 relations between the Algonquins and the Jamestown settlers were very strained. Powhatan was holding several English prisoners, and the colonists were in desperate need of corn which they believed the Indians had in abundance and could afford to share with them. Furthermore, the English believed that some of their stolen weapons were still in the hands of Powhatan. Therefore, the English decided to kidnap Pocahontas and hold her hostage until they got what they wanted from her father. She was kidnapped by a sea captain, Samuel Argell, in 1613 and taken to Jamestown where she was apparently well treated. While she was being held captive she was instructed in the teachings of Christianity, converted and baptised. She was given the Christian name Rebecca. A number of writers have expressed the opinion that she was a good and true Christian; how she really felt about her adopted religion only she knew.

While Pocahontas was being held in captivity, she met and possibly fell in love with John Rolfe, a 39-year-old religiously devout widower. He was an English gentleman with contacts at court. It is quite amazing, considering the usual attitude of the English to the Indians, that a man with such a background wanted to marry Pocahontas, princess or not. He wrote a long and rambling letter to the colonial governor in which he tried to explain and justify his desire to marry the young Indian girl. He insisted the reason was not lust. Perhaps thinking that the marriage would foster peace with the Indians, the governor gave his approval.

However, the main concern of most of the men in Jamestown was to get Powhatan to ransom his daughter and agree to a new peace pact. A message was sent to Chief Powhatan demanding the return of the English prisoners, a large amount of corn, and the return of the stolen weapons. Powhatan met the first two demands but not the third, so the English refused to return Pocahontas to her people. There were no further negotiations for several months. Finally, in the spring of 1614, Captain Argell led a delegation up the river to Powhatan's headquarters to try to reopen negotiations with the chief in person. One of the two men sent to speak with him was John Rolfe. Powhatan refused to see the delegates, but he did permit his brother

Apachamo to talk with them. Apachamo promised the Englishmen that he would try to persuade his brother to agree to a peaceful settlement between the two sides. The English then felt compelled to return without further delay to Jamestown because it was time for spring planting. They did warn Apachmo, however, that if a settlement was not reached by autumn, they would return after their harvest was collected and wage all-out war against the Indians. Such an attack would undoubtedly have resulted in a great loss of lives on both sides.

Shortly thereafter, Powhatan learned that John Rolfe, the English gentleman, wanted to marry his daughter. The chief may have seen the proposed marriage as a face-saving and peaceful means of settling his differences with the colonists or perhaps he was flattered that an English gentleman wanted to marry his daughter. He quickly gave his consent, sent one of Pocahontas' uncles to represent him at the wedding and sent two of his sons to attend. He also sent the bride a present of fresh-water pearls and gave the couple a considerable amount of land on the James River for their new home. Most importantly, he agreed to settle all remaining differences with the settlers at Jamestown. The couple were married that same spring (1614).

The marriage may have prevented the loss in battle of many lives. Relations were good between the settlers and the Algonquins in the years following.

Not much is known about John Rolfe. We do know that he was very interested in the development of the colony, was highly respected by his peers, and was the first English colonist to plant tobacco in America. He served as the first Secretary and Recorder-General in Virginia and was later a member of the governor's council. This is one case in which the name of the husband was overshadowed by that of the wife.

30. Pocahontas, painted in England in 1616.

Rolfe and Pocahontas had one child, a son named Thomas. While the boy was still an infant, Pocahontas and Rolfe were invited by Governor Dale to travel to England with him when he went home in 1616. Dale may have had an ulterior motive for inviting the Rolfes to travel with him: the government in London was fed up with the trials and tribulations of the Virginia Colony and was becoming indifferent to its fate; Pocahontas was expected to create quite a sensation in London. She would also be seen as an example of how thoroughly the colonists were converting the heathens to Christianity. Because an American Indian princess would be such a novelty in London, she was sure to attract a lot of attention and would perhaps revive interest and support for the Virginia Colony. Advance notice was sent to London extolling the deeds and virtues of the princess. Captain John Smith wrote his letter to Queen Anne, telling her of how Pocahontas had saved his life and of her many services to the colony.

Pocahontas was treated royally in London. She was the first American woman to be presented to the English royal court. She was included in the royal party when it attended the Globe theatre to see Shakespeare's *The Tempest*. Whenever she and her husband went into the street, people gathered to stare. On arrival she had been tutored in proper behaviour and was highly praised for her decorum. The English sometimes referred to her as Lady Rebecca. Unfortunately, we have no idea of what Pocahontas thought of London or Londoners. It is known that she could not tolerate the damp English climate, and was soon suffering from ill health.

The Rolfes had been in England for seven months when John received word that he had been appointed Secretary and Recorder-General of the Virginia Colony. He was anxious to return and take up his new position, so he and his wife prepared to sail for home. Their ship was still anchored in the Thames when Pocahontas became critically ill, and she died at the age of twenty-two. By some accounts she died of tuberculosis; others say it was smallpox. She was buried in an unmarked grave in Gravesend, England, and her death is listed in the parish register simply as the wife of John Rolfe, gentleman. Rolfe left his young son in London with an uncle and returned to America.

Although we know nothing of Pocahontas' life from her own point of view, and much of what we have learned from others has been embellished and possibly distorted, she is still an historic figure of some significance. Her life was unique in the time in which she lived. She did many good deeds and her progeny made many significant contributions. Her marriage to John Rolfe brought years of good relations between the Virginia Colony settlers and the Algonquins. Her relationship with Captain John Smith had always been of interest to many people. These are some of the reasons for presenting this brief biography of her life. Our final objective is to show how the third generation of her descendants linked up with the Eldridges.

Pocahontas' and John Rolfe's son Thomas returned to Virginia when he was about twenty-five. He prospered as a landowner, married Jane Poythress, and left one daughter named Jane. It is interesting to note that Thomas made several visits to his Indian relatives. We do not know the date of his death.

Jane Rolfe married Colonel Robert Bolling who had come to America from England when he was about fifteen. He was of a prominent old English family whose ancestral home was Bolling Hall near Bradford. In Virginia, he prospered in commerce, trading both with his fellow countrymen and with the Indians. He also served as a member of the House of Burgesses. Jane and Robert Bolling had five daughters and one son – the great-grandchildren of Pocahontas.

In about 1727 one of the Bolling daughters, Martha, married Thomas Eldridge, a lawyer, thus uniting an Eldridge with a direct descendant of Pocahontas. The children of this marriage were, of course, direct descendants of Pocahontas. She was their great-great-grandmother. Thus, from about 1730 onwards, the Eldridges of this line are descendants of one of the best known women in American history, the Indian princess Pocahontas.

Note: *This chapter was written by Catherine Smiley Bartlett, B.S. in Education; M.A. in history.*

Chapter Twelve

Nelson Beardsley Eldred III

Colonel Nelson Beardsley[10] Eldred III is a descendant in the 10th generation from Samuel Eldred.

Samuel[1] Eldred (1620-97) **m**. Elizabeth Miller.
Captain John[2] Eldred (1659-1724) **m**. Margaret Holden (1663-1740).
Robert[3] Eldred (c.1705-c.1758) **m**. Hannah Rathbone (1706-*c*.1764).
James[4] Eldred (1740-1808) **m**.1. Lucy Reynolds (1743-1802).
                  2. Joanna (Reynolds) Wilson,
                    sister of Lucy (1755-1832).
Robert[5] Eldred (1761-1844) **m**.1. Sarah Boone (1761-1832).
                  2. Sarah Burdick.
Charles Boone[6] Eldred (1799-1871) **m**. Matilda Spink (1804-57).
Nicholas Boone Spink[7] Eldred (1824-78) **m**. Marietta Beardsley (1827-1915).
Nelson Beardsley[8] Eldred (1852-1931) **m**. Emma Georgina Caldwell (1867-1945).
Nelson Beardsley[9] Eldred, Jr. (1893-1975) **m**. 1. Charlot Louise White.
                    2. Dorothy Ethel McCool.
Nelson Beardsley[10] Eldred III **m**. Joan Alice Smiley.
Charles Nelson[11] Eldred **m**. Linda Hazel Mitchell.

Samuel[1] Eldred (1620-97)
He was born on 27 November 1620 in Ipswich, England, and married Elizabeth Miller there on 25 November 1640. The parish register of St Mary-at-Quays, Ipswich, reads: 'Nov. 25, 1640, Married, Samuel Eldred of Ipswich, cordwainer, and Elizabeth, daughter of Daniel Miller, of Needham Market'. He died between 13 April 1697 and 12 February 1699 in the town of Kingstowne, Rhode Island.

Samuel and Elizabeth (Miller) Eldred appear in Cambridge, Massachusetts in 1641; according to one source they had left Bristol, England, on 23 March 1641 on the *Tiger* bound for Boston. In documents of the time the surname is usually spelt Eldred, Eldredge, or Eldridge.

Samuel Eldred and his family spent their first years in America in Massachusetts Bay Colony living in various places near Boston, Cambridge, Charlestown, Chelsea and Medford. At first he was a shoemaker, and later he farmed rented land. In 1660 the family moved to Stonington, Connecticut, and later to Wickford on the western shore of Narragansett Bay in R.I. where many of Samuel's descendants lived for the next 100 years. As a constable in Wickford, under the authority of Connecticut, Samuel was in the very centre of the political troubles of the Narragansett Colony and this caused him much grief.

While in Boston he joined the 'Ancient and Honourable Artillery Company of Massachusetts' from 1641-49.

Known Children of Samuel and Elizabeth (Miller) Eldred

1. **Elizabeth[2]**, **b**. 26 October 1642, Cambridge, Mass., probably died young. NFK.
2. **Samuel[2]**, **b**. 2 October 1644, Cambridge, Mass.
   > **m**. Martha Knowles (*c*.1651-1728) daughter of Henry and Elizabeth (Potter) Knowles of Portsmouth and Warwick, R.I.
   > **d**. 1720 Kingstowne, R.I.
3. **Mary[2]**, **b**. 15 June 1646, Cambridge, Mass.
   > **m**. Rouse Helme, son of Christopher and Margaret Helme.
   > **d**. 17 May 1712, Kingstowne, R.I.
4. **Thomas[2]**, **b**. 8 September 1648, Cambridge Mass.
   > **m**. Susanna Cole (*c*.1653-1726), daughter of John and Susanna (Hutchinson) Cole, and grand-daughter of William and Anne (Marbury) Hutchinson. Her grandmother Anne (1591-1643) was a martyr of religious liberty and an early settler in R.I.
   > **d**. 1726, North Kingstowne, R.I.
5. **James[2]**, **b**. *c*.1650, probably at Cambridge, Mass.
   > **m**. no record.
   > **d**. *c*.1687.
6. **John[2]**, of whom below
7. **Daniel[2]**, **b**. *c*.1663, Wickford, R.I.
   > **m**. Mary (Phillips?) *c*.1687
   > **d**. 18 August 1726, North Kingstowne, R.I.

John[2] Eldred (1659-1724)

He was born 17 August 1659, probably at Chelsea, Mass. His family moved to R.I. when he was a year old and he grew up in the Narragansett Colony. In the records he spelt his name Eldridge. John was chosen Ensign in Kingstowne Militia; he was subsequently promoted to Captain. In May 1696 he was admitted a freeman of the colony. He was elected treasurer of Kingstowne in 1697. In 1707 he was a member of the Town Council and a Deputy in 1708. He married Margaret Holden (1663-1740), daughter of Randall and Frances (Latham) Dungan. She was the daughter of Lewis Latham, Falconer to King Charles I of England. John died 17 September 1724, at North Kingstowne, R.I.

Known Children of John and Margaret (Holden) Eldred

1. **James[3]**, **b**. *c*.1683, Kingstowne, R.I.
   > **m**. name of wife unknown, will proved 11 April 1768.
2. **Thomas[3]**, **b**. *c*.1685, Kingstowne, R.I.
   > **m**. Rebecca Downing 26 March 1730, North Kingstowne, R.I.
   > **d**. unknown.
3. **Samuel[3]**, **b**. *c*.1693, Kingstowne, R.I.
   > **m**. Content Rathbone, 25 May 1712. She was born 17 January 1692 at New Shoreham (Block Island), R.I., a daughter of Captain Thomas and Mary (Dickens) Rathbone, died after 29 August 1769 as she was mentioned in son John's will of that date.

d. 1764, West Greenwich, R.I.
4. **Margaret**[3], **b**. *c*.1699, Kingstowne, R.I.
  m. 1. William Gardner (Gardiner) 12 June 1718. He was born
  27 October 1697, son of Henry and Abigail (Remington) Gardner
  (Gardiner). His will, in which Margaret is mentioned, is dated
  10 October 1731. The estate was settled on 8 May 1732.
   2. Isaac Austin, 26 December 1736, died after 1779.
5. **Anthony**[3], **b**. 1700.
  m. Joanna – .
  d. 1758, will proved 22 January 1759.
6. **William**[3], **b**. *c*.1700, Kingstowne, R.I.
  m. Lydia, died 16 February 1739 (date of account to Town Council by
  widow, Lydia).
  d. at North Kingstowne, R.I.
7. **Barbara**[3], **b**. after 1703, Kingstowne, R.I.
  m. Major John Albro after 1726.
  d. unknown.
8. **Abigail**[3], **b**. *c*.1704, Kingstowne, R.I.
  m. Samuel Rathbun (Rathbone) in 1736. His will was proved 14 February
  1786. He mentions his grandson, Roger Rathbun, who married Mary
  Eldred, daughter of Seth Eldred.
  d. unknown.
9. **Robert**[3], of whom below.

Robert[3] **Eldred** (*c*.1705-10-*c*.1758)
He was born between 1705-10 in North Kingstown[1], R.I. He married Hannah, daughter of Joseph and Mary (Mosher) Rathbone (Rathbun) who was born 12 March 1706. Her will was proved on 12 February 1764. She was the granddaughter of John and great-granddaughter of Richard Rathbone (Rathbun). Documentary entries include:

20 Feb. 1717/18	Received 45 acres of land from his father.
1718	Made freeman.
1731-36	Ensign of North Kingstown's Second Company of Militia.
1736	He is called 'Vinter' in court records.
1755	Called innkeeper in court records.

Robert Eldred's will was recorded 10 July 1758, and his wife's will was proved 12 February 1764. Son James and son-in-law Eber Sherman were executors.
Known Children of Robert[3] **and Hannah (Rathbone or Rathbun) Eldred**
(All born in North Kingstowne, R.I.).
1. **Margaret**[4], **b**. unknown
  m. Eber Sherman in February 1738/9 at South Kingstown. He was
  born on 7 August 1719.
  d. unknown.

1 Kingstowne changed to Kingstown around this time.

  2. **John**[4], **d**. young.
  3. **Simeon**[4],**d**. young.
  4. **Abigail**[4], **b**.1723.
        m. Thomas Remington (19 August 1723-12 April 1808) on 14 December
        1744.
        d. 14 April 1766.
  5. **Thankful**[4], **b**. unknown.
        m. Daniel Scranton on 22 September 1744 at North Kingstowne.
        d. unknown.
  6. **William**[4], **m**. Phoebe. NFK.
  7. **Hannah**[4], **b**. July 1734.
        m. John Rathbone (Rathbun) (1737 - 1 June 1818).
        d. 10 June 1821.
  8. **Mary**[4], **b**. 9 September NFK.
  9. **James**[4], of whom below.
10.**Barbara**[4], **b**. 21 July NFK

James[4] **Eldred** (1740-1818)
He was born on 29 August 1740 at North Kingstown, R.I., and died there on 3 April 1818. He married 1. Lucy, daughter of George and Joanna (Spencer) Reynolds. She was born on 8 July 1743 and died on 8 September 1802. George Reynolds was the son of Jospeh and grandson of James Reynolds. James[4] Eldred married 2. Joanna (Reynolds) Wilson – the sister of his first wife Lucy – on 8 June 1803. She was born on 12 March 1755 and died on 27 May 1832 at Warwick, R.I.
Known Children of James[4] **and Lucy (Reynolds) Eldred**
(All born in North Kingstown, R.I.)
  1. **Robert**[5], of whom below.
  2. **George**[5], **b**. 18 March 1763.
  3. **Christian**[5], **b**. 16 November 1764.
  4. **Charles**[5], **b**. 5 May 1766.
        d. September 1782.
  5. **Daniel**[5], **b**. 5 January 1768.
        m. Mary Phillips, 10 January 1797.
  6. **Nancy**[5], **b**. 9 September 1769.
        m. 1. James Boone Peckham, 2. – Spink.
        d. 14 April 1843.
  7. **Joanna**[5], **b**. 10 July 1771. Twin to Hannah.
  8. **Hannah**[5], **b**. 10 July 1771.
        m. Benjamin Northup, the widower of her sister Phoebe Ann.
  9. **Lucy**[5], **b**. 28 August 1774.
        m. James Gardiner.
        d. 18 September 1802.
10. **Beriah Brown**[5], **b**. 21 March 1776.
        m. 1. Elizabeth Peckham, 7 September 1800, 2. Phoebe Reynolds
        (3 February 1788/9-September 1829) on 29 April 1807.
        d. 12 November 1844.

11. **Clark**[5], **b**. 2 December 1777,
       d. at sea.
12. **Phoebe Ann**[5], **b**. 17 November 1779,
               m. Benjamin Northup, 14 March 1799, North Kingstown, R.I. He
               was born 10 April 1777, North Kingstown, R.I. and died
               18 December 1856, Deerfield, N.Y., son of Capt. William and Ann
               (Slocum) Northup and grandson of Nicholas (Stephen) and
               Freelove (Eldred) Northup. They had six children, all born in
               Deerfield, N.Y.
               d. 21 September 1809 at Deerfield, N.Y.
13. **Rowland**[5], **b**. 4 October 1781.
        d. at sea.
14. **Mary**[5], **b**. 25 November 1787.
        m. John Capron, 4 December 1804.

Robert[5] **Eldred** (1761-1844)
He was born 23 October 1761 at North Kingstown, R.I., and died there on 12 November 1844. He married 1. Sarah Boone, daughter of James Boone, on 1 January 1789. She was born on 3 June 1763 and died on 6 December 1832. He married 2. Sarah Burdock, the illegitimate daughter of Phoenix Brown and the widow Abigail (Eldred) Burdock. She survived him and married as her second husband Richard Smith.

Robert was a sea captain in early life, and later kept a tavern and a store at Wickford, R.I. He served as a private in the militia under Captain William Taylor, Captain John Cole and others during the Revolution and as a substitute for his father, enlisting eight times between 1776 and April 1780. He was a lieutenant of the North Kingstown Fourth Company of Militia in 1785, first lieutenant of the Rangers in 1788 and 1789, a surveyor for the Port of North Kingstown in 1790, and Justice of the Peace from 1817-37. Upon his application dated 12 November 1832 he was granted a Revolutionary War pension (S21746).

Other documentary entries include:

Robert Eldred and Sarah his wife, and Mary Boone, Widow, all of North Kingstowne, R.I., sold to Nicholas Spink and William Gardner, land and dwelling house bounded south on Twenty Rod Highway – said land belonging to Mr. Samuel Boone, dec'd. 1793.

His will was dated 19 December 1840, and is recorded on probate records of Kingstown, R.I. He makes bequests to his wife, Sarah B. Eldred, of the house and lands in the village of Wickford during her lifetime, and to his son Robert certain lands which after Robert's death are to go to 'his son William, my Grandson'.

    To daughter, Mary U. Tillinghast.
    To son, Richard Boone Eldred, $100.
    To son, Charles Eldred.
    To James Boone Tillinghast, Clark Peckham Tillinghast, and Lodowick Hoxie Tillinghast, sons of my daughter, Abby Tillinghast, dec'd.

To daughter, Susan Hoxie.

To daughter, Sarah B. Waite.

Also, to daughter, Mary U. Tillinghast, wife of George Tillinghast, the small trunk that was her grandmother Boone's.

To granddaughter, Sarah Boone Tillinghast.

To grandson, Robert Eldred, son of my son, Richard B. Eldred.

To Richard Boone Eldred, William Eldred and John Eldred, sons of my son Robert Junr.

Known Children of Robert[5] and Sarah (Boone) Eldred

(All born in North Kingstown, R.I.)

1. **Susanna Boone**[6], **b**. 5 October 1789.

> **m**. 1. George Washington Tillinghast, on 4 September 1806, at North Kingstown. He was a manufacturer and brigadier general (3 July 1783-7 October 1827) son of George and Mary (Greene) Tillinghast.
>
> 2. William King Hoxie of Newport, R.I. in 1833.
>
> **d**. 2 September 1885,

2. **James Boone**[6], **d**. 30 October 1793, aged 17 months.

3. **Sarah Boone**[6], **b**. 28 May 1794.

> **m**. 1. Hutchinson Cole who died 12 September 1820, aged 31, on board the brig *Agenora*.
>
> 2. Joseph Waite who died 20 June 1855 aged 67 years.
>
> Issue by first husband: **i. Susan Cole**, who married Captain Thomas Holloway
>
> **ii. George Hutchinson Cole**, who **d**. 3 May 1880 at Wickford. He **m**. Eliza Malissa Crombe (3 July 1826-10 June 1910) on 18 September 1848.
>
> **d**. 30 October 1863.

4. **William**[6], **b**. 21 April 1795,

> **m**. Louisa Northup on 3 January 1820 who died 30 August 1821 in her 27th year of 'childbed fever'.
>
> Issue: **i. Augustavus Eldred** (29 July 1821-6 August 1821).
>
> **d**. in February 1822 at Smithville, North Carolina.

5. **Charles**[6], of whom below.

6. **Robert**[6] **Jr.**, **b**. 17 December 1800.

> **m**. Martha Smith, a daughter of Richard and Mary Smith, on 27 June 1824.
>
> She was born on 11 June 1807 and died in November 1862.
>
> Issue: **i. William Boone Eldred**, **b**. 9 February 1826, **m**. Elizabeth Clark Sweet (11 March 1829-1912) on 13 December 1850 and died in 1913.

    ii. John Robert Clark Eldred, b. 10 December 1827,
       m. Abby Frances Rathbun (15 September 1830-13 June
       1915) on 13 June 1847.
       d. 20 January 1892.

7. **Richard Boone**[6], **b**. 2 January 1803,
      m. Nancy Lord Chesebrough (10 July 1811-30 May 1892),
      a daughter of Ezra and Sally (Palmer) Chesebrough of
      Stonington, Conn., on 22 January 1832.
      Issue: **i. Charles Boone Eldred** (5 May 1834-4 September 1887),
        unmarried.
        ii. Robert Eldred (10 December 1837-17 October 1838).
        iii. Edwin Chesebrough Eldred (15 March 1836-23 January
         1873), **d**. in Capetown, South Africa, unmarried.
        iv. Robert Eldred, born 29 August 1839,
         m. Charlotte A. Smith on 6 December 1883.
        v. Sarah Eldred, born 22 October 1841, **m**. James Noyes
        Chesebrough.
        vi. Abigail Eldred (9 February 1844-21 December 1851).
        vii. Andrew Jackson Eldred (8 February 1846-17 December
         1854), **m**. Maria Virginia Hutardo on 7 October 1883.

8. **Mary Updike**[6], **b**. 24 January 1806.
      m. George Tillinghast (born 15 January 1803), a son of William
      and Eleanor (Baker) Tillinghast; they migrated to Berlinville,
      Ohio.
      Issue: **i. Sarah Eldred**
        ii. Rebecca Eldred
        iii. Mary Eldred
        iv. Frederick Eldred

9. **Abigail Goddard**[6], **b**. 25 December 1808/9, died 27 March 1836.
      m. Nicholas Tillinghast (30 March 1807-18 August 1891,
       at Providence, R.I.) in 1828. He was a brother of
       George who married Mary Updike[6].
      Issue: **i. James Boone Eldred b.** 18 April 1830
        m. Ellen Ford and lived in Decorah, Iowa.
        ii. Clark Peckham Eldred (9 May 1832-7 February 1913)
        iii. Lodowick Hoxie Eldred b. 16 June 1834
         m. Eliza Peck.

Charles[6] **Eldred** (1799-1871)
He was born in Wickford, R.I., on 2 September 1799 and died on 30 April 1871. He married Matilda Spink (15 March 1804-5 June 1857) on 29 June 1820 in North Kingstown, R.I. She was the daughter of Nicholas (1781-1862) and Hannah (Potter) (1784-1860) Spink.

Known Children of Charles and Mathilda (Spink) Eldred:
1. Hannah Matilda Spink Eldred, (2 September 1821-1 October 1854)
2. Nicholas Boone Spink Eldred, of whom below. The family settled in Auburn, New York, and are buried in the Fort Hill cemetery of that city.

Nicholas Boone Spink[7] Eldred (1824-78)
He was born in North Kingstown, R.I., on 19 November 1824. He attended Hobart College in Geneva, N.Y., and Union College at Troy. N.Y., before graduating in 1846 with an B.A. degree. He settled in Auburn, N.Y., but did not engage in business. Being scholarly by nature and an ardent devotee of books, he acquired an excellent library, indulging his zest for knowledge and culture until his death on 3 July 1878. He married Marietta Beardsley (born in Auburn on 5 October 1827 and died there on 15 January 1915) on 5 June 1849. She was the daughter of John Beardsley (1783-1857) and Alice Booth, who was born on 22 December 1786. Both Nicholas and Marietta are buried in the Fort Hill cemetery in Auburn.
Known Children of Nicholas and Marietta (Beardsley) Eldred:
1. Nelson Beardsley Eldred, (1852-1931), of whom below.
2. George Field Eldred, (1857-1926).
3. Gertrude Eldred, b. Ohio *c.*1870.

Nelson Beardsley[8] Eldred (1852-1931)
He was born in Auburn. N.Y., on 16 May 1852, and died there on 26 April 1931. He married Emma Georgina Caldwell (14 June 1867-28 January 1945) on 28 September 1892 at Auburn. She was the daughter of George Sage Caldwell (1833-1916) and Arabella Theodosia Corwin. Mr. Eldred, who was a life resident of Auburn, was managing director of the Nelson Beardsley estate, a director and chairman of the board of the Cayuga County National Bank, vice president of the Auburn Savings Bank, and an official with the Auburn Water Works. In his youth he was noted as an athlete, particularly as an oarsman; he was affiliated with the Cayuga County Historical Society, and was prominent in civic and social affairs. Mrs. Eldred, who was born in Syracuse, N.Y., spent most of her life in Auburn, and was an acknowledged society leader. Both are buried in the Fort Hill cemetery in Auburn.
Known Children of Nelson and Emma (Caldwell) Eldred
1. Nelson Beardsley Eldred, Jr. of whom below.
2. Margaret Caldwell (Eldred) McIntosh (22 June 1895-26 December 1935) **m.** John McIntosh (1890-1930).
3. Katharine (Eldred) Hutchinson (24 May 1897-2 November 1978) **m.** J. Dana Hutchinson (1896-1967).
4. Rosamund (Eldred) Hurlburt (25 June 1900-1974) **m.** John B. Hurlburt (1895-1974).

Nelson Beardsley[9] Eldred, Jr. (1893-1975)
He was born in Auburn, N.Y., on 25 December 1893, and died in Grosse Pointe Farms, Michigan, where he had lived for many years, on 30 September 1975.

He married 1. Charlot Louise White (9 September 1899-1 February 1983) of Brookline, Mass., daughter of General and Mrs. James Gardiner White of that city. James Gardiner White (22 May 1860-7 February 1929), was Commissary General of Massachusetts and widely known in military and insurance circles. He married Margaret Mattocks (21 June 1873-29 January 1958) on 17 September 1896. She was the daughter of General Charles Porter Mattocks, a Civil War hero and holder of the Congressional Medal of Honour, who lived in Portland, Maine.

Charlot married Edgar DeWitt Jones, Jr. (21 November 1902-20 August 1983) on 18 April 1942.

Nelson married 2. Dorothy Ethel McCool (27 March 1906-to date) on 22 June 1945. She was the daughter of John Franklin McCool and Frances Edna Fox; Dorothy now resides in Grosse Pointe Farms.

Nelson attended the public school in Auburn until 1908, and then St Paul's School in Concord, New Hampshire (1909-1913). He joined the New York National Guard in 1916, entered active federal service in 1917, and served in France as an infantry officer during the First World War, specializing in machine gun tactics and operations. After the war he lived in various New England and Midwestern states, working initially as an automobile executive, and later as an officer in the rubber manufacturing industry.

Known Children of Nelson and Charlot (White) Eldred
1. Nelson Beardsley Eldred III, of whom below.
2. Margaret Mattocks (Eldred) Rabey of Bakersfield, California. She is married to Theodore Warren Rabey.
> Issue: **i. Marcia Elaine Ginn.**
> **ii. Theodore Warren Rabey, Jr.**
> **iii. Sandra Jean Weisel.**
> **iv. George Alan Rabey.**

Nelson Beardsley[10] Eldred III (1925-to date)
He was born in Jamaica Plain (near Boston), Mass., on 13 March 1925. He married 1. Elynlea Robinson on 29 May 1948, she is the mother of their twin daughters. He married 2. Glen Jenkins Kennedy on 19 February 1953, she is the mother of their son. He married 3. Joan Smiley of Tiffin, Ohio on 21 December 1962. Joan is a school teacher, graduate of Georgia State University, and genealogist of the Smiley family.

Nelson attended Culver Military Academy, Culver Indiana (1939-43) and served in the United States Army (1943-73). His military service included the Second World War, Korea and Vietnam, and foreign tours of duty in the Far East, Middle East and Europe. He retired with 30 years of service as a Colonel, Adjutant General Corps. Among his awards and decorations are the Legion of Merit (1st Oak Leaf Cluster), Bronze Star Medal, and Army Commendation Medal. He attended the University of Texas and is a member of the Phi Gamma Delta Fraternity, the Honorable Order of Kentucky Colonels, the U.S. Army Infantry Hall of Fame, the Sons of the American Revolution, the Ancient and Honorable Artillery Company of Massachusetts and several genealogical and historical societies. Nelson and Joan reside in Marietta, near Atlanta, Georgia.

Known Children of Nelson and Elynlea (Robinson) Eldred

1. Ellen Mercedese (Yaun). Born 14 May 1949, in San Antonio, Texas. She **m.** Dr. Michael Ryan and they live in Kansas City, West Missouri. Ellen is a graduate of the University of Texas, holding a masters degree and a degree in law.

2. Lea Margaret (Yaun). Born 14 May 1949, in San Antonio, Texas. She **m.** Robert Kugle and they live in San Antonio. Lea is a graduate of the University of Texas, holding a masters degree. *The twins were legally adopted by Elynlea Robinson's second husband, Claude Yaun.*

Known Children of Nelson and Glen (Jenkins Kennedy) Eldred

1. Charles Nelson Eldred, of whom below.

Charles Nelson[11] Eldred

He was born at Fort Belvoir, Virginia, 4 December 1953. He is married to Linda Hazel Mitchell, born 17 May 1947, in Fitzgerald, Georgia. She is the daughter of Thomas Hazel (1918-77) and Edna Mildred Mitchell (née Pope).

Charles attended Culver Military Academy, Culver, Indiana (1968-72), Drake University, Des Moines, Iowa (1972-74), and the University of Georgia, Athens, Georgia (1974-76) where he graduated with a Bachelor of Business Administration degree. He is a member of the Phi Delta Theta Fraternity. Upon graduation, Charles joined the Georgia Power Company and is manager of Cash Planning and Operations. In 1990 he was recognized by the Georgia Power Accounting and Finance Association as the Professional of the Year. In June 1991, Charles earned a Masters in Business Administration, with a concentration in finance, from Mercer University, Stetson School of Business and Economics. In 1992 he was named Manager of the Year by the Georgia Chapter of the National Management Association. Charles is a member by right of descent (Samuel Eldred 1641-49) of the Ancient and Honorable Artillery Company of Massachusetts. He also serves as a member of the of the Board of Directors for the Scottish Rite Festival Foundation and the State of Georgia Arthritis Foundation.

His wife, Linda, attended Georgia Southern University and has been employed in banking circles for some time, mainly in personnel and accounting departments. They live in Roswell, Georgia.

Known Children of Charles Nelson and Linda (Hazel) Eldred

1. Joseph Eldred, an adopted son, born 7 January 1969.

2. Jennifer Eldred, born 29 April 1980.

3. Stephen Eldred, born 20 June 1988.

31. Nelson Beardsley Eldred III.

Chapter Thirteen

John Trevor Eldrid

John Trevor[6] Eldrid is a descendant in the sixth generation from Thomas Eldrid, founder of a family business in the City of London, eventually known as Eldrid, Ottaway and Company of 53 Whitecross Street and 1-3 Silk Street of Cripplegate, manufacturers and suppliers to the wholesale and export trade of saddlery, harness, leather and sports goods.

Cripplegate is an area within the City of London which straddles the line of the old Roman wall, half a mile to the north of St Paul's Cathedral. Here, until it was demolished in 1760, stood a fortified gate, beyond which in the Middle Ages was a watch-tower or 'burgh-kenning', linked to the gate by a covered way or 'creppel'. The first gave its name to the post-war development of the Barbican; the second was corrupted into Cripplegate.

Thomas[1] Eldrid (1770-1833) **m**. 1. Mary Briscoe (1770-1821).
                                          2. Nancy Stubbs (1773-1866).
Thomas[2] Eldrid (1797-1860) **m**. Mary Ann Stubbs (1802-75).
John[3] Eldrid (1827-79) **m**. Caroline Hodges (1829-93).
John[4] Eldrid (1856-1945) **m**. Emily Ann Laws (1855-1933).
John[5] Eldrid (1883-1971) **m**. Violet Elizabeth Juanita Borrajo (1882-1968).
John Trevor[6] Eldrid (b. 1916) **m**. 1. Berylle Hillier Hawkins.
                                          2. Nathalie Chatham Beauclerk.
                                          3. Blanche Evelyn Cairns.
Paul Trevor[7] Eldrid (1956-57).

Thomas[1] Eldrid (1770-1833)
He was born *c*.1770, probably in the Birmingham area. In about 1794, he married Mary Briscoe, who was born in 1770 and bore him six children. In 1800, he set up a business at 53 London Wall as a coach plater and brass founder. Shortly afterwards, a firm of hemp merchants, saddlers and ironmongers, trading under the name of Henry Clifton Atkinson, removed from Snow Hill, near Newgate prison, where the frequent hanging of felons probably created a steady demand for their products, to new premises at 21 Fore Street. Fore Street backs onto London Wall, and by 1810 John Atkinson and Thomas Eldrid were in partnership at the Fore Street address.

The business prospered, as well it might at a time when the horse was still man's major means of transport. By the time of his death in 1833, at Highbury Terrace, Islington, then a fashionable, semi-rural suburb north of the metropolis, Thomas Eldrid was comfortably off, and his life was insured with the Hope Insurance Company for the sum of £1,000. In his will, dated 12 October 1832, Thomas nominated two relatives to be his executors: Thomas Eldrid, his eldest son, and John Stubbs, his

son-in-law and a Birmingham solicitor, both of whose sisters married Eldrids –
Elizabeth to Edward Eldrid, brother of Thomas[1], and Mary Ann to Thomas[2].

Thomas[1] was buried in the churchyard of St Giles, Cripplegate, as was his first wife.
His younger children and many of his grandchildren were baptised in the same
church. Of all the buildings which stood in this area when Thomas[1] was alive, only
St Giles' church, a survivor of both the Great Fire of 1666 and the German air raids
during the Second World War, remains, together with sections of the old London
wall.

Known Children of Thomas and Mary (Briscoe) Eldrid

1. **Mary Ann**[2], **b.** 1795
        d. 1827. NFK.
2. **Thomas**[2], of whom below.
3. **George**[2], **b.** 1799. NFK.
4. **Louisa**[2], **b.** 1801. NFK.
5. **Edward**[2], **b.** 1803 in London, worked for the family business in Cripplegate and,
        like brother Thomas, was admitted to the Drapers Company.
        m. Elizabeth Hards (1817-90) in 1827. Edward separated from his wife in
        1867 and went to live in Turnham Green, Middlesex.
        d. 1870.
        Issue: **i. Edward Hards**, a veterinary surgeon who practised in Horsham
                and Sevenoaks (1829-90).
                Issue: **1. Thomas Edward**, **b.** and **d.** in 1858.
                       2. Miriam Fanny, **b.** 1861 **m.** 1878. NFK.
                       3. William Francis, **b.** 1864. NFK.
                       4. Christian Edward, **b.** 1867. NFK.
                       5. Constance Louisa, **b.** 1870. NFK.
                       6. Edward, **b.** 1871. NFK.
            ii. Fanny, (1830-1874).
            iii. Louisa, (1833-1859).
            iv. Francis Augustus (1836-1850).
6. **Eleanor b.** 1814.
        m. 1871. NFK.

Thomas[2] **Eldrid** (*c.*1797-1860)

He was born *c.*1797 in Middlesex. In 1822 he married Mary Ann Stubbs (1802-75), of
Walsall, Staffs., who was his stepmother's daughter. Thomas inherited his father's
interest in the firm of Atkinson and Eldrid and, through the good offices of his
business partner, John Atkinson, a member of the Worshipful Company of Drapers
of the City of London, both he and his younger brother, Edward, were admitted by
servitude to the Freedom of the Company and, later, to the Livery. Thomas took
up his entitlement to the Freedom of the City and, in due course, was elected to
represent Cripplegate Without on the Court of Common Council.

In 1838, the family business became known as Atkinson, Eldrid and Sons, but in
1851 Atkinson's name was dropped altogether and the name of the firm became
John Eldrid and Co. Meanwhile, Thomas Eldrid and John Atkinson continued their
partnership in London's fashionable West End, trading as Atkinson and Eldrid,

Whipmakers, at 185 Regent Street, and Thomas removed from Islington to a smarter house in Ladbroke Square. But this arrangement was short-lived. After 40 years in the City, Thomas felt it was time to retire, so he bought a house in Guildford, Surrey, to which he moved in 1854. He died six years later and was buried in the churchyard at Stoke.

Known Children of Thomas and Mary Ann (Stubbs) Eldrid
All born in Islington and baptised in St Giles, Cripplegate.

1. Mary Ann[3], **b**. 1824. NFK.

2. Thomas Stubbs[3], **b**. 1826.
                m. 1861.
                d. 1874.

3. John[3] of whom below

4. Edward Henry[3] **b**. 1828. Merchant banker, was associated for 50 years with the Spanish-owned Murietta's Bank in Old Broad Street in the City of London. In 1893, the bank was in grave difficulties and, although retired Edward came to the rescue of his former employees with a large injection of funds from his own private fortune.
        m. 1862, Sarah Jane Crickmer, daughter of Charles Crickmer, wine merchant, of 19 Camden Grove, Kensington, from whom he inherited a legacy of £3,000.
        d. 1905, leaving an estate valued at £43,000. His wife died in 1913; the couple had no children. Edward was a Liveryman of the Drapers Company.

5. Emily[3], **b**. 1830.
          m. 1853. NFK.

6. George[3], **b**. 1834.
          d. 1868.

7. Joseph Walter[3], **b**. 1836   **d.** 1904
        m. 1. Frances Row Anderson (1841-1900) daughter of George Anderson, a surgeon of Guildford.
        Issue: **i. Walter Henry St John**, **b**. 1866. May have emigrated to Canada.
               ii. Maitland Ross   **b**. 1868   **d.** 1935
              iii. Mary Beatrice, b. 1870   **m.** 1889.
              iv. Ethel, b. 1869. NFK.
               v. Gordon Heath, b. 1874, alive in 1935. Emigrated to America in 1895
               m. Irma Velten of Milwaukee, Wisconsin.
               Issue: **1.   Gordon (or Gerald) Eldrid, b**. 1899 in New York City. Gordon Heath and his wife were on the professional stage.
             vi. Renault Holden, b. 1877, **m**. 1. Dorothy Florence Odell.
              Issue: **Mignonne Dorothy, b**. 1899.
        m. 2. Annie Dee (1866-1939) in 1900. She was the daughter of Joseph William Dee, accountant, of Knowle, Warwickshire.

Issue: **1. Gladys May**, **b**. 1892.
      2. Phyllis Madge, b. 1903.
      Both married and had issue.

Joseph Walter Eldrid joined his brothers, John and Thomas Stubbs Eldrid, in the family business. From 1865 until 1881, when ill-health occasioned his early retirement, he was, in fact, the sole proprietor. He became a member of the Drapers Company and, like his father, Thomas, served on the Court of Common Council and as secretary of the Cripplegate Ward Club, both of which offices he resigned in 1882. He lived for some years in Sidcup, Kent, where, according to his son, Gordon Heath Eldrid, he was active in local affairs. He was certainly churchwarden at his local church and was present when a petition touching the interests of his parish was laid before the Archbishop of Canterbury. He came out of retirement to work for a pharmaceutical firm, and after living at various addresses in the south of England, he finally settled in the city of Worcester.

8. Catherine Eliza[3], **b**. 1840.
      m. 1876. NFK.
9. Edwin Norton[3], **b**. 1842. Ordained a priest in the Church of England. Met his wife whilst serving as a curate in a Derbyshire parish. She was Agatha Gisborne who came from an old established Derbyshire family who had connections with Mary Shelley and Lord Bryon. They married in 1869 in Derby and he became curate-in-charge at the 15th century church of St Ethelburga in Bishopsgate, London. The church still stands, one of the oldest buildings in the city, predating the Great Fire of 1666, where, it is said, a post-Reformation minister was nailed to the pillory by his ears for saying Mass after its abolition. The rector, who commanded a stipend of £1,000, had retired from the scene and appointed Edwin Eldrid to run the church for a miserly £140 a year. Hard working and reliable, Edwin revived the church's flagging fortunes. In 1883, the bishop of London instructed his chaplain to write and congratulate him on his success. Nevertheless, he aroused much criticism for his 'high church' practices, and there was an acrimonious exchange of letters in the City press between those who opposed and those who supported him.

Issue: **i. Michaelangelo Sacheverel de la Pole**
      (1876-1957). Served in the South African police,
      married twice.
  ii. Mary Selina (1878-1910).
  iii. Valentine Byron Curzon (1880-1958). A civil servant, in 1924
      m. Jesse Brown.
      Issue: **John Eldrid, b**. 1925, who took Holy Orders and now
      directs the London branch of the Samaritans, a service to help
      the lonely and suicidal. It was founded by the Rev. Chad Varah,
      and has its headquarters in the basement of St Stephens' church,
      Wallbrook, in the City of London.
      John **m**. Miss Green in 1954.
      Issue: **1. Sarah Eldrid, b**. 1955.
            2. Peter John Eldrid, b. 1957.
  iv. Agatha Gabrielle, b. 1882 **m**. 1906. NFK.
Edwin Norton Eldrid **d**. 1893 in Dorking, Surrey.

John[3] Eldrid (1827-1879)

He was born in Islington in 1827 and died in Fellows Road, Hampstead, in 1879. In 1853 he married Caroline Hodges, whose sister, Sarah, was the mother of London businesssman Frank Isitt, who married the international ballerina, Adeline Genée, D.B.E. (1878-1970), a Danish girl who was not only one of the best and most loved dancers of her day, but one of the founders of modern British ballet. Adelaide, another of Caroline's sisters, was born in 1830, not long after the death of George IV (the erstwhile Prince Regent), lived through four reigns and died at the age of 101 in 1931. She was a remarkable woman who, in a sense, spanned in her own lifetime the six generations of the Eldrid family recorded in this chronicle: Thomas[1] did not die until she was three years old, and the present writer, John Trevor[7] well remembers meeting her when he was a schoolboy.

Known Children of John[3] and Caroline (Hodges) Eldrid

1. **John[4]**, of whom below.
2. **Arthur[4], b.** 1858 in London.

 m. Gertrude Rosina Reynolds in 1887. Arthur began his career as a clerk in the same merchant bank in Old Broad Street as his uncle, Edward Henry Eldrid, and in 1889, was admitted to the Livery of the Drapers Company. In 1893 he decided to seek his fortune abroad, and with his wife and young family emigrated to Valparaiso, Chile. But he died within four years of his arrival in South America. His widow remarried and together with her four sons, settled in Argentina, where her children were educated.

 Issue: **i. Arthur Allen, b.** 1888 in England. Arthur Allen

   m. Francisca Blanc.

   Issue: **1. Alice Nancy.**

    2. Esther Fanny.

    3. Arthur Leslie, m. Lilian Harding.

     Issue: **Alan Andrew, b.** 1961 in Tandil, Argentina.

      Muriel Paula, b. 1964 in Tandil, Argentina.

  ii. John Leslie, **b.** 1890 in England. He was killed in action in the Battle of the Somme in 1916.

  iii. Norman, **b.** 1891 in England.

  iv. Cedric, **b.** 1894 in Chile. Information about Cedric is meagre. He married and died before 1943.

  Issue: **Norman**

   Joan, both of whom in their turn married and had issue.

3. Mary Anne[4], **b**. 1859.
  m. 1881 Frank Snelling, a London businessman.
  d. 1930.
  Issue: **i. Florence Mary.**
     ii. Beatrice Georgina.
    iii. Christine.
    iv. Irene.
     v. Isabel.
    vi. Carrie Gwendoline.
   vii. Vera Maud.
    All were born before the turn of the century. Florence, Beatrice, Christine and Irene married. Florence **m**. Wellesley Tudor Pole.
    Issue: **1. Jean Leslie**, **m**. 1951 Sir John Carroll, Scientific Adviser to the Board of Admiralty, by whom she had a son and a daughter.
     2. Christopher, married with issue.
     3. David, married with issue.
    Beatrice **m**. Harold Moore, no issue.
    Christine **m**. Dr. A. Magill, no issue.
    Irene **m**. Stanley Mann (former partner in the London philatelic firm of Stanley Gibbons).
    Issue: **1. Colin**
      2. St John.
    Of Mary Anne's family of seven daughters, Carrie is now the only survivor and attained her hundredth birthday in May 1992.
4. Edward Cotterill[4], 1860-61.
5. Walter Percy[4], **b**. 1862 in Islington,
  m. Alice Howes in 1889. Walter was a chartered accountant, and practised first at 46 Holborn Viaduct and later at Old Jewry Chambers. In February 1899 he was declared bankrupt in the London Bankruptcy Court. Shortly afterwards, and as a consequence of this, he resigned from the Livery of the Drapers' Company which he had joined in 1889.
  Issue: **i. Kathleen** (1890-1933).
     ii. Walter Thorne, **b**. 1892. NFK.
      d. 1924. After his death, his widow and daughter lived in Braunton, Devon.
6. Annie Maud[4], **b**. 1865.
  m. Sana 1915. NFK.

John[4] **Eldrid** (1856-1945)
He was born in 1856 at 21 Fore Street, Cripplegate, within earshot of Bow Bells and, as such, could claim to be a genuine Cockney. He was baptised at St Michael's church, Cornhill, the advowson and patronage of which was vested in the Drapers

Company in 1503. In a church of the same name and on the same site that was later to be destroyed during the Great Fire of London, an earlier John Eldred had married Joan Walley, and their five children were all baptised there between the years 1570-81. Buried in that earlier church was Edmund Eldred, son of Nicholas of Knettishall, a Freeman of the Merchant Taylors' Company, who died of the plague in 1569. His servant, Ralph Bulman, also died of the plague five months after his master.

John[4] married Emily Ann Laws in 1881 in St Saviours church, South Hampstead. Emily Laws (1855-1933) was the eldest daughter of Charles Laws (1833-1874) an architect, and Jane Laws (nèe Bennett), and was born at 12 Doughty Street, Mecklenburgh Square, London. This was the street of handsome Georgian houses, still standing, where in 1837 at no. 48, Charles Dickens began his married life, although he was no longer living there when Emily was born. The famous novelist's house is preserved as a Dickens museum. Emily's sister, Louisa, married Heinrich Theune, a merchant from Stettin, then in Germany, now Poland, and her younger brother, Charles Frederick, ran away to sea in the days of sail, and rose to be a captain on ships of the Royal Mail line. During the First World War he was master of a troop-carrying ship which was torpedoed by the German navy. He died in Eastbourne in 1936 aged seventy-four.

In 1881, on the retirement of his uncle, Joseph Walter Eldrid, John[5] inherited the family business. He took as his partner a senior warehouseman, V. Austen Ottaway, and the business, which had moved to new and larger premises in Whitecross Street three years earlier enjoyed a long and settled period of progress. Despite the arrival of the railways, there was still, as a trade paper of the time put it, 'nothing like leather', and it went on to say that, of the many organic substances utilized by man, the skins of animals variously prepared, had in all ages been the most important and useful, and in the present day, leather with all its extensive applications, was more valuable than ever. In that favourable climate, John Eldrid, supported by his sons, John and Ernest, the firm of Eldrid, Ottaway and Company prospered, there being hardly a town in England where they did not have a retail outlet for their products.

John Eldrid retired before the outbreak of the Second World War, and after the destruction of his family home in Hampstead, he went to live in Potters Bar, Hertfordshire, where he died in 1945, aged ninety.

He was a freeman of the City of London, and of the Drapers Company, of which, at the time of his death, he was Senior Liveryman.

Known Children of John[4] and Emily Ann (Laws) Eldrid

1. Muriel[5], **b**. 1882 at Chiswick.
> **d**. 1973 at Potters Bar. Nursed with the British Red Cross during the First World War.

2. John[5], of whom below.

3. Emily[5], **b**. 1886 at Fellows Road, Hampstead.
> **m**. Henry Edmund Goodwin in 1935.
> **d**. 1970 at Potters Bar. Became a fluent German speaker and kept in close touch with her German cousins. No issue.

4. Ernest Edward[5], **b.** 1887 at Fellows Road, Hampstead. Served in the British Army during the First World War and was wounded on the Western Front. He was in the family business of Eldrid, Ottaway and Company. Ernest was a good club cricketer; a skilful slow bowler, he is on record as having claimed the wicket of the famous Surrey and England player, Jack Hobbs.
d. 1958

John[5] **Eldrid, Jr** (1883-1971)
He was born in 1883 in Chiswick and educated in London and Bedford. He joined his father in the family business at the turn of the century. Following the First World War, he developed a sports and fancy leather department to offset the decline in the demand for harness and saddlery goods brought about by the arrival of the motor car. The business suffered during the trade recession of the 1930s, and was dealt a hammer blow when the whole of its premises, stock and records was destroyed by enemy action during an air attack on London in the winter of 1941-42. John Eldrid and his colleagues, undaunted by this disaster, acquired other premises from their neighbours, Whitbreads Brewery, and with the help of a friendly trade competitor, John Bliss, were soon back in business. A year later, the firm was commissioned to make a set of saddlery as a birthday gift for the Russian wartime leader, Marshal Timoshenko. Described as a credit to the craftsmanship of British saddlers, the gift was presented to the Russians at the Empress Stadium in Earls Court.

In 1950, the firm celebrated its bicentenary, for it was in 1750 that the Atkinson family began the business which Thomas Eldrid joined in 1810. At the celebratory dinner an important guest was John Bliss, with whose firm, Eldrid Ottaway had amalgamated in 1953 This was the first in a series of mergers during which the family name disappeared. Nevertheless, the current brand name 'Eldonian' used by Allied English Saddlery and Leather Goods Ltd. uses the first three letters of 'Eldrid' and appeared in the name of a competition in the Horse of the Year Show as the Eldonian Double Harness Scurry.

In 1913 he married Violet Elizabeth Juanita Borrajo (1882-1968), the eldest daughter of Eduardo Marto Borrajo (1853-1909), Librarian to the Corporation of the City of London and curator of the Guildhall museum.

Issue: **John Trevor Eldrid**, of whom below.

Eduardo Borrajo's father His Excellency Senor D. José Borrajo (1797-1887) was President of the Spanish Financial Commission in London and Paris. Mr. Eduardo Borrajo was born in Ramsgate, Kent, of an Irish mother. In 1897 he helped to organise the International Library Conference at Guildhall, London, working with the Lord Mayor of London, the Marquess of Bute and Sir Henry Irving to prepare a brilliant entertainment for the delegates. Mr. Borrajo, a member of the Worshipful Company of Cutlers, died at sea off Melbourne, during a voyage which he had taken for his health. His wife, Rhoda (nèe Smyth) was born in 1855 and lived to become a nonagenarian. Their eldest son, Edward Joseph Borrajo M.B.E. was deputy chairman of the Prudential Assurance Company of Great Britain.

John Eldrid died at Sutton, in Surrey, in 1971, at the age of eighty-eight. Like his father he was a staunch and loyal member of the Drapers Company, of which he, also, had the distinction of being the Senior Liveryman.

John Trevor[6] **Eldrid** (1916-to date)
He was born in London in 1916, the year of the Battle of the Somme on the Western Front in France. He was educated in London and followed his uncle into the employ of the Prudential Assurance Company because at that time (1933) the future of the family business was uncertain. During the Second World War he served with the British Army in England and the Middle East where in addition to his military duties he regularly broadcast news bulletins in English on Egyptian State Broadcasting. His interest in all facets of publicity and public relations, including theatre and film, found an outlet in his work for the Prudential after the war. He travelled throughout Britain and wrote extensively for the company's various publications. Interest in other countries led him to travel widely outside Britain when the opportunity arose. He retired as a senior executive of his company at the end of 1981 and is now pursuing his various interests, including genealogy, in retirement.

The City of London has always figured amongst these interests and, in his view, the history of England is mirrored in the history of its capital city. He became a freeman in 1937, at the age of 21, and was admitted to the Livery of the Drapers Company in the City of London in 1943. As he was then on active service overseas, his father stood proxy for him at the admission ceremony. He was the first member of his family to be elected to the Court of Assistants, the Company's governing body, which occurred in 1976. Ten years later he was Master, the first Eldrid to be Master of one of the 12 senior companies of the City of London since John Eldred of Great Saxham became Master of the Clothworkers in 1604. There is, of course, a link between the Clothworkers and the Drapers: both companies were concerned with different facets of the wool trade – England's staple industry during the Middle Ages.

During his year of office, he attended many functions on behalf of his company, the most memorable and historic being the service at St Paul's Cathedral to commemorate the Silver Jubilee of Queen Elizabeth II, followed by luncheon at Guildhall at which the Queen delivered her speech of re-dedication to her loyal subjects.

In 1981, Trevor Eldrid attended some of the ceremonies in Virginia, U.S.A. marking the bicentenary of the Battle of Independence. In Washington he gave a lunchtime talk to members of the Great American Achievements Program, outlining the sympathetic position taken by the City of London towards the colonists in that bitter struggle. In London in 1982 he represented the Master of the Drapers' Company at the victory parade in the City of London to honour the British Task Force after its victory in the South Atlantic.

He has married three times. His first wife was Berylle Hillier Hawkins (1921-71), his second Nathalie Chatham Beauclerk (née Walker), (1915-1975) previously married to the 13th Duke of St Albans. His present wife is a New Zealander, Blanche Evelyn Cairns (née Ayre) who was born in 1928.

Known Children of Trevor and Nathalie (Chatham Beauclerk) Eldrid
        Issue: **1. Josephine Helen**, **b.**1952,
               2. Paul Trevor, **b.** 1956 **d.** 1957

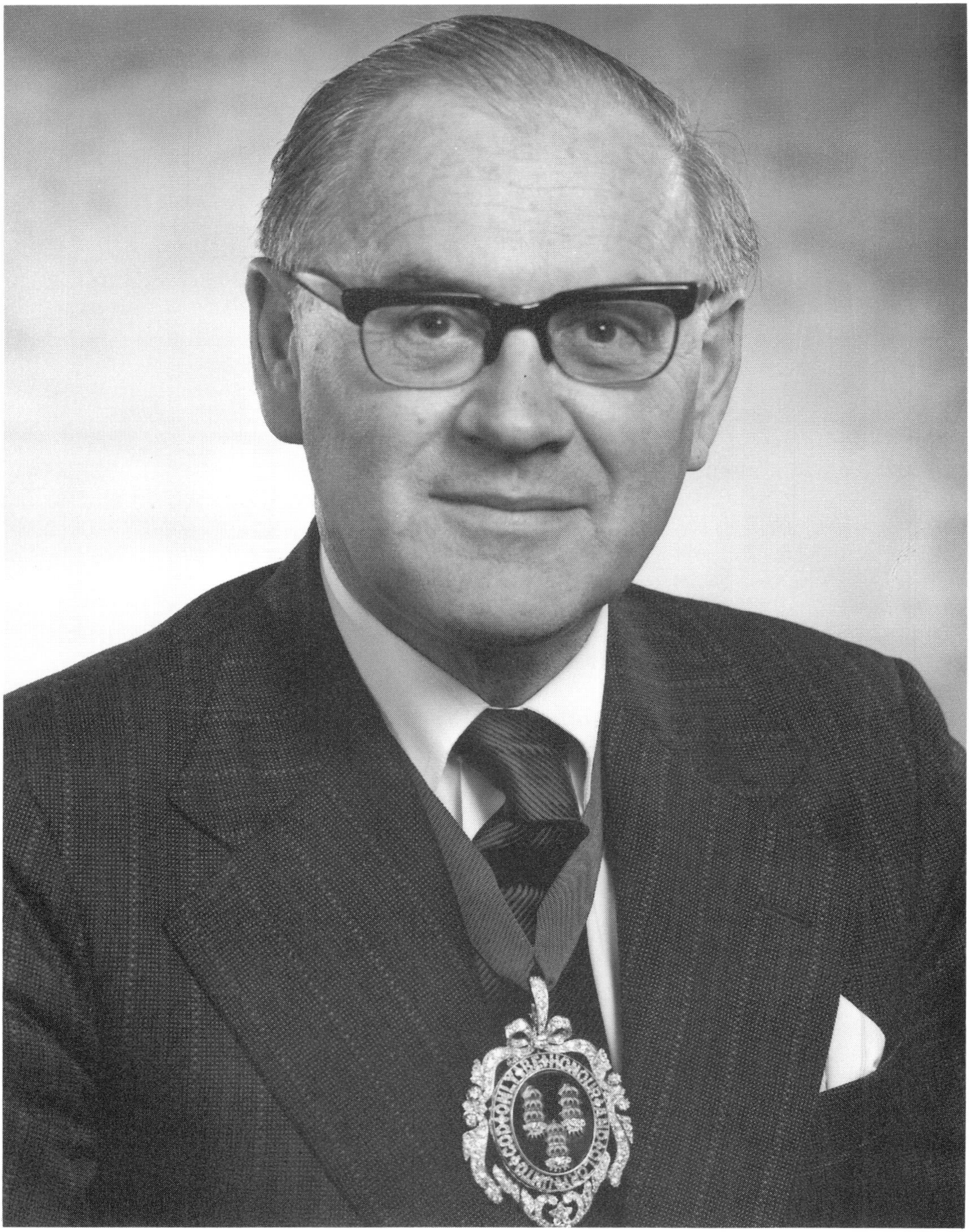

32. John Trevor Eldrid.

Appendix I

The Cargo of the Hercules

Port of London Port Book, f.I, Entry 9, E 190 8/I, Public Record Office.

Inventory of Cargo

Undecimo die Aprilis 1588

Cl. Hercules de London oneris
  250 Dlb [?tons].
Richard Parsons – magister ab
  Tripoli
C. Sir Edward Osborne, Richard
  Stapers, etc., pro:

xlvi bales rawe Silke at vmxii
  lb. great weight.
xiii bales synamon at iimciiiixvi lb.
liiii bales barcke of Synamon
  caled scavesons at 101 clb. weight.
Ciiii balles nutmegges at
  iiiclxxiii clb. weight.
iiclxvii balles Indico 528
  clb. weight.
i bale cloves at ciiii lb.
ii bales Salarmoniack at
  iiiiclvi lb.
ii bales et dimidium fustes of
  cloves at iiiiclvi lb.
ii bales mirabolans at iiclvi lb.
ii bales maces at iiiicxxviii lb.
xxxiii bales pepper at
  lxviiciiii lb.
i boxe at xxx lb. China.
ii bales Sanguis Draconis at
  iiclx lb.

ii bales aloes epatica at
  iiiclx lb.

Translation

11th day of April 1588

Vessel – the *Hercules* of London,
  weight 250 tons [?].
Master – Richard Parsons from
  Tripoli
Owners: Sir Edward Osborne, Richard
  Stapers, etc. for:

46 bales of raw silk at 5,012 lbs.
  great weight.
13 bales of cinnamon at 2,196 lbs.
54 bales of bark of cinnamon ... at
  101 cwt.
180 bales of nutmegs at 373 cwt.

267 bales of indigo [dye] at
  528 cwt.
1 bale of cloves at 104 lbs.
2 bales of salamoniac [ammonium
  chloride used for bleach] at 456 lbs.
2½ bales of cloves at 466 lbs.

2 bales of mirabolans at 256 lbs.
2 bales of mace [spice] at 428 lbs.
33 bales of pepper at 6,780 lbs.

1 box at 30 lbs. of China.
2 bales of dragons' blood [resin
  orgum from palm fruit used in
  medicines and for dyeing] at 260 lbs.
2 bales of aloes [drug from aloe plant
  used as liver purgative] at 360 lbs.

xxiii botanes of cotton cloth at
   xvciiii x peces.
xi bales wattred and unwattred
   Chamblettes at viclx single
   peces.

Iiii balles grogranies at
   xviiclxx dooble peces.

i boxe mirre at xxiii lb.
ii bales callamus at iiiicxx lb.

xxxi balles cotton yerne at lxxvi clb.
iii bales Shasshes at vcxviii
   peces.

xxv peces Iser cloth.
ii balles Comashes at lv peces.

ix balles woormeseed at xv clb.

iiciiii bagges galls at 416 clb.
   weight.

liii Sackes cotton wooll at 155 clb.
i balle at ix quittes of cotton cloth.
i bale scamonie at cx lb.

i bale at xiii turky Carpettes.
iiii bales ginger at vcl lb.
ii bales moma at iii clb.

x bales casia fistola at xicxx lb.

ix bales longe pepper at
   xiiiicxx lb.
v Chests mastick at vi clb.

i bagge Sponges at c lb weight.

Valor xxxviimdciiii iii li. iiis. viiid.

Subsidia mdcciiii iiii li. iiis. iid.

23 bundles [?] of cotton cloth at
   1,590 pieces.
11 bales of watered and unwatered
   camlets [fabric made of silk and
   camel's hair or angora goat] at
   660 single pieces.
53 bales of grograms [coarse silk mixed
   with mohair and often stiffened with
   gum] at 1,770 double pieces.
1 box of myrrh [used in perfume] at 23 lbs.
2 bales of catamus [medicinal plant]
   at 420 lbs.
31 balls of cotton yarn at 76 cwt.
3 bales of sashes [fine linen or silk
   worn as turbans in the East] at
   518 pieces.
25 pieces of Iser cloth.
2 bales of comashes [kind of cloth]
   at 55 pieces.
9 bales of wormseed [used in medicine
   as a vermifuge] at 15 cwt.
203 bags of galls [nutgalls used for
   making ink, dyeing and in medicine]
   at 416 cwt.
3 sacks of cotton wool at 155 cwt.
1 bale at 9 quittes [?] of cotton cloth.
1 bale of scammony [plant resin used
   as a strong purgative] at 110 lbs.
1 bale of 13 turkish carpets.
4 bales of ginger at 550 lbs.
2 bales of moma [unknown substance]
   at 3 cwt.
10 bales of cassia fistula [cinnamon
   oil used as a mild laxative] at 1,120 lbs.
9 bales of long pepper at 1,420 lbs.

5 chests of mastic [tree resin used
   as glue] at 6 cwt.
1 bag of sponges at 1 cwt.

Value £37,683 2s. 8d.

Duty £1,784 3s. 2d.

Manor of Great Saxham (Saxham Hall)

11th century
St Edmund

St. Edmund

The parish of Great Saxham (Saxham Magna or Sexham) belonged to the Saxon Britulf, son of Leomar. He also owned Little Saxham and Chevington. Dispossessed by William the Conqueror, his lands were given to the monastery of St Edmund. Some land near Frizzeler's (Fresel's) Green and Herstwood was granted partly to the Abbot and partly to the priory of nuns at Thetford.

14 Edward I
(1272-1307)

Edmund de Hemegrave, Walter Fresel, and others held land in Great Saxham from the abbot.

7 Edward III
(1327-77)

Sir Edmund de Hemegrave and his son, Sir Thomas, enfeoffed Edmund de Mutford with their manor of Great Saxham called Wodethorp Hall. Sir Thomas' feoffees sold the manor to Thomas Hethe of Hengrave, who later sold it to Humphrey, Earl of Stafford.

3 Edward I
24 Edward III
41 Edward III
44 Edward III

Fresel

Walter Fresel, son of Ralph, held lands in Westly called Fresel's Manor; Richard Fresel was Bailiff of Clare (3 Ed. I); Sir Richard Fresel was Knight of the Shire (24 Ed. III); Sir Richard's daughter, Agnes Fresel, released all her inherited lands in Saxham after her brother Richard's death, to Henry, son of William de Hethe (41 Ed. III). Agnes and Thomas de Scoles (her first husband) released all rent and services due from Henry on these lands (44 Ed. III). The family manor in Great Saxham was located near Herstwood and Fresel's Green.

33 Henry VIII
(1509-47)

The Fresel Manor in Great Saxham belonged to the priory of nuns at Thetford. It was granted to Thomas Skipwith (of St Alban's) and Sir Nicholas Bacon (Solicitor-General, later Lord Keeper) by the Crown (33 Hy. VIII). Thomas Skipwith released his rights and Sir Nicholas Bacon sold the property to Sir Clement Heigham of Barrow.

25 Qn. E.I.
(1558-1603)

Sir Clement Heigham's son, Sir John, sold the Fresel Manor to Thomas Bacon of Hesset; then it passed to John Morley, and from him to Sir Thomas Kytson.

33 Henry VIII

Long
Kytson died 1546

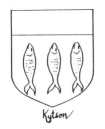

The manor of Great Saxham with the advowson of the church was part of the dissolved monastery of St Edmund and was granted to Sir Richard Long and his wife Margaret. He was the younger (third) son of Sir Thomas Long of Wraxell and had married Margaret, widow of Sir Thomas Kytson of Hengrave, later titled the Countess of Bath. Sir Richard was a royal favourite, a gentleman of the Privy Chamber, Master of the Buckhounds and Hawks, High Steward, and Captain of the Islands of Guernsey and Jersey. His son, Henry Long, married Dorothy Clerke with the king as a sponsor. Their only daughter, Elizabeth, married William Lord Russell, father of the 4th Earl of Bedford. As there was no male heir, the manor reverted to the Crown.

Qn. E. I

31 Qn. E. I

Various parts passed quickly through several courtiers, including the Earl of Leicester. The manor and advowson were finally bought by Sir Thomas Kytson of Hengrave, who now held the entire mentioned properties acquired by the abbot and nuns in the 11th century.

1597

8 James I
(1603-25)

Sir Thomas Kytson sold the manor and advowson at Great Saxham for £3,000 to John Eldred (1556-1632) of London. He later bought Herstwood from Sir Thomas and his wife Elizabeth for £800 as parkland.

John Eldred was an alderman in London and a Levant merchant of considerable enterprise and renown. He married Mary Revett (Rivet) and built an Elizabethan manor house, sometimes known as Nutmeg Hall (J. E. introduced nutmegs into England).

Eldred died 1632

He was succeeded by his eldest son, Sir Revett (Revit) Eldred, Bt., who married Anne Blakwey of Salop. Sir Revett died without issue, and the manor and lands were inherited by Lady Anne Eldred, his widow. She remarried, but on her death left the manor and properties to John Eldred's great-nephew John

1745
Mure

Mure

Eldred, who married Elizabeth Hervey. The latter and their son, John, died about the same time, and the place was sold to Hutchinson Mure, a younger son of the Mures of Caldwell, Renfrewshire.

1774

The house, which was in the style of James I, with five gables and a centre porch, was altered and enlarged by William Adams.

1779

Great Saxham Hall burned down accidentally and a new one (the centre portion of the present house) was built near the original site in 1780.

1795

After the death of Hutchinson Mure in 1794, his widow and son and heir sold the estate to Thomas Mills.

1798

Mills

Mills

Thomas Mills, D.L., J.P., High Sheriff of Suffolk, finished building the present house, employing Joseph Patience, probably a pupil of Soane. The drawings of this and the previous alterations are in the Soane Museum. It is possible that Mure may have intended the octagonal room to be a central hall with the staircase under the painted ceiling. Thomas Mills largely rebuilt St Andrew's church, Great Saxham, originally 12th-century. The tower and porch, mid-15th-century, were not altered.

d. 1834
d. 1865

Thomas Mills died, leaving his widow Susannah Harris; his eldest son, William Mills, D.L., J.P., succeeded him and married Clare Huntley.

d. 1884

1896

William's son, Thomas Richard Mills, High Sheriff, married Emily Hall. His son, also Thomas Richard Mills, sold the estate to Charles Morley.

1912

William Firth bought the manor, built a wing to the north-east basically for servants' accommodation, and put in the present stairs. Beset by financial problems, the estate was taken over by a consortium which divided it into smaller parcels.

1922

Stanley

Stanley

Brigadier, the Right Honourable Frederick Stanley, P.C., M.C., M.P., 2nd son of the 17th Earl of Derby, purchased the manor and lands that constituted Great Saxham Hall.

1927

Magnay

Sir Christopher Magnay, Bt., grandson of a lord mayor of London, purchased the estate and pulled down the Firth additions. After his widow's death, it was bought by General Sir William Stirling, G.C.B., C.B.C., D.S.O.

1967
Stirling
1981

Stirling

A description of Saxham Hall furnished by Lady Stirling, the present owner, provides current information on this historic estate located five miles from Bury St Edmunds, Suffolk: 'The Eldred house was more or less on the same site as the present one, though it faced north and south while my house is east and west. The present house has five entertaining rooms, including a long drawing or ballroom, and octagonal drawing room under the dome – 11 bedrooms. The estate is now 500 acres of which 300 is farming land and the rest woodland, with a small shoot, pheasants, partridge, hares and rabbits. Great Saxham is located about a mile from Saxham Hall to the north, the church (St Andrew's) is about 200 yards from the house; and there are some cottages to the south'.

Appendix III

St Andrew's church, Great Saxham, Bury St Edmunds, Suffolk, England

St Andrew's church is located about two hundred yards from Saxham Hall. The original structure was built in the 12th century; only the north and south circular style doors remain from this period. The tower and porch date from the mid-15th century, and the rest of the church is comparatively new, having been rebuilt in 1798 by Thomas Mills, High Sheriff of Suffolk and owner of Saxham Hall until his death in 1834.

This small country church contains some 16th-century European coloured window glass of rare quality etched with intricate religious scenes, a 15th-century font, and a Jacobean pulpit. The parish registers start in 1555 and entries on early members of the Eldred family can be found.

John Eldred (1556-1632) of Great Saxham and London is buried near the altar. There is a coloured bust of this prominent merchant-adventurer and alderman of London in a circular niche on the south side of the church. An engraved brass memorial on the chancel floor depicts him in his alderman's gown surrounded by the coats of arms of Eldred, Eldred-Revitt, Revitt (his wife's family), the City of London, Clothworkers' Guild, East India and the Russia Companies. There are three inscriptions, one of which states that the memorials were erected by his son and heir, Revett Eldred, in 1632.

139

Dedication from William Eldred's Survey of Dover

To the most noble and gracious Lord James Duke of Richmond, Earl of March, etc., Constable of Dover Castle, Lord Warden, Chancellor and Admiral of the Cinque Ports, to the ancient towns and their members, Knight of the Most Noble Order of the Garter and one of His Majesty's most honourable Privy Council (and to the rest of the Honourable and Worshipful Commissioners for Dover Harbour).

Right Honourable, Honourable and Right Worshipful Commissioners for Dover Harbour, for as much as from the first grant of this harbour lands unto this day I have been employed in measuring and plotting all these lands, as well as in general, by which the first grant was passed from the King to my Lord of Northampton, as also being commanded all the first sittings of this honourable session to measure and make plots of each man's several ground which I have carefully observed since the time of the first sessions unto this present. And that now I have lived by God's providence to see all lands granted in lease which have passed through my hands by plots to render an account of this my command I have carefully collected all these plots as well the general plot of Dover Harbour, the Town and Castle, as also every man's several ground into this book in which general plot you may see the situation of the town and harbour and in the particular plots every man's land as it is granted to the several tenants. Beginning at the ancient gate of Dover called Snargate and so along under the cliff to Archcliff Bulwark and from the cliff to the low water mark of the sea, with each man's name that owneth the ground, the number of foots contained on each plot in length and breadth, how it boundeth upon another, and how it is situated toward the south or north, with the name of the street where it lieth, also for the better understanding of this work on the other side of the leaf is written in red letters the tenants' names of the first grant and against them the names of those tenants that now this present year holdeth these lands, the number of foot on each side and the situation south or north with the name also of the street where it lieth, which book I have presented unto all this honourable sessions which now are and always have been so careful for the benefit of the harbour, to the intent it may remain to succeeding ages which will be then in more use than it is now, and thus recording this my work and pains to your wise and honourable considerations, my time and labour in his world being now at an end, with my humble and hearty prayers to God for the health and prosperity of My Lord Duke's Grace and the rest of this honourable sessions. I humbly rest at your service to be commanded.

WILLIAM ELDRED

Chart I: Eldred of Great Saxham

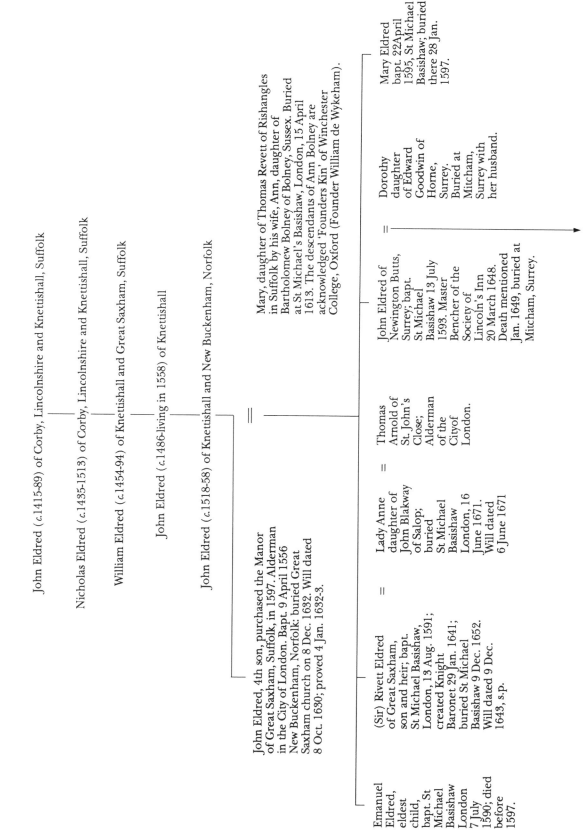

John Eldred (c.1415–89) of Corby, Lincolnshire and Knettishall, Suffolk

Nicholas Eldred (c.1435–1513) of Corby, Lincolnshire and Knettishall, Suffolk

William Eldred (c.1454–94) of Knettishall and Great Saxham, Suffolk

John Eldred (c.1486–living in 1558) of Knettishall

John Eldred (c.1518–58) of Knettishall and New Buckenham, Norfolk

Mary, daughter of Thomas Revett of Rishangles in Suffolk by his wife, Ann, daughter of Bartholomew Bolney of Bolney, Sussex. Buried at St Michael's Basishaw, London, 15 April 1613. The descendants of Ann Bolney are acknowledged 'Founders Kin' of Winchester College, Oxford (Founder William de Wykeham).

John Eldred, 4th son, purchased the Manor of Great Saxham, Suffolk, in 1597. Alderman in the City of London. Bapt. 9 April 1556 New Buckenham, Norfolk: buried Great Saxham church on 8 Dec. 1632. Will dated 8 Oct. 1630; proved 4 Jan. 1632-3.

Emanuel Eldred, eldest child, bapt. St Michael Basishaw London 7 July 1590; died before 1597.

==

(Sir) Rivett Eldred of Great Saxham, son and heir; bapt. St Michael Basishaw, London, 13 Aug. 1591; created Knight Baronet 29 Jan. 1641; buried St Michael Basishaw 9 Dec. 1652. Will dated 9 Dec. 1643, s.p.

==

Lady Anne daughter of John Blakway of Salop; buried St Michael Basishaw London, 16 June 1671. Will dated 6 June 1671

==

Thomas Arnold of St John's Close; Alderman of the City of London.

John Eldred of Newington Butts, Surrey; bapt. St Michael Basishaw 13 July 1598. Master Bencher of the Society of Lincoln's Inn 20 March 1648. Death mentioned Jan. 1649, buried at Mitcham, Surrey.

==

Dorothy daughter of Edward Goodwin of Horne, Surrey. Buried at Mitcham, Surrey with her husband.

Mary Eldred bapt. 22 April 1595, St Michael Basishaw; buried there 28 Jan. 1597.

Genealogical chart (Eldred family).

Top generation (children):

- **Elizabeth Eldred**, bapt. St Michael Basishaw 27 June 1596. Died after 1627.
  = (1) (Sir) Edward Wortley Miles.
  = (2) (Sir) Samuel Tryon of Lower Marney, Essex. Died 28 March 1627, buried at Halsted; will proved 26 Apr. 1627.

- **Anne**, bapt. St Michael Basishaw, London, 25 Feb. 1598.
  = Robert Henley Bencher of the Middle Temple.

- **Benjamin Eldred**, bapt. St Michael Basishaw 21 Jan. 1604. Died before his father (1632). s.p.

- **Joseph Eldred**, bapt. St Michael Basishaw 28 Oct. 1608; buried 17 March 1609.

- **Joseph Eldred**, bapt. 28 Jan. 1609, St Michael Basishaw LLB, Fellow of New College, Oxford. Died 5 Nov. 1645, s.p.

- **Mary Eldred**, Bapt. St Michael Basishaw 15 April 1613.
  = Miles Corbet, son of Thomas Corbet of Sprouston Norfolk.

Children of Anne Eldred and Robert Henley:

- **Robert**, b. c.1623, Protho-Notary of the Common Bench; grandfather of Rober Henley.
- **Mary**, bapt. at Great Saxham 29 Jan. 1625.
- **(Sir) Andrew** b. c.1621, of Bramshill, Southampton. Created a Bt. 30 June 1660.

Lower generation:

- **John Eldred** of Knightsbridge, Middlesex; b. c.1632; died before 1671.
  = Charity, daughter of Sir Jacob Rivers of Chafford, by his wife Charity, daughter of John Shirley of Isfield, Sussex. Married (2) Thomas Lee of Cotton, Salop.

- **Thomas Eldred**, Parish of St Margaret Westminster; b. c.1634; died Westminster in 1691.
  = Margaret, daughter of Walter Sanchey (Sankey), merchant of London.

- **Anna** b. c.1619.
- **Florence**, b. c.1621.
- **Elizabeth**, b c.1623.
  all died in infancy.

- **Dorothy Eldred**, b. c.1625. Had issue.
  = Thomas Lee of Lincoln's Inn; barrister 1673.

- **Ann Eldred**, chr. c.1627, married Launcelot Lee 1663. Had issue.

- **Mary Eldred**, b. c.1630; married John Mitchell of Newington Butts, Surrey. Had issue.

John Eldred of Great Saxham; b. 1664, Knightsbridge Middlesex, died 1 March 1725, buried. Great Saxham = Elizabeth, 2nd daughter of Francis Hervey, *alias* Mildmay of Marks, Essex; b. 1770; m. 7 April 1687; buried Great Saxham, 23 June 1742.

Thomas Eldred, age 7 in 1673; died young. s.p.

John Eldred of Bury St Edmunds; b. 1661, prob. at Newington, Surrey; will proved 18 Nov. 1712. = Anne

John Eldred of Great Saxham; b. 30 Aug. 1691 bapt. at Great Saxham 19 Sept. 1691; buried there 23 March 1746. Will dated 21 Aug. 1745, s.p. = Anne, buried at Great Saxham, 1 Feb. 1747.

Charity Eldred, bapt. Great Saxham, 16 Aug. 1688.

Dorothy Eldred, b. 30 Jan. 1689; bapt. at Great Saxham, 19 Feb. 1689.

Note: the manor and advowson of Great Saxham were sold to Hutchinson Mure, Esq., a younger son of the Mures of Caldwell, Renfrewshire, in 1745. The manor house was accidentally burned down in 1779 and was rebuilt a year later near the original site.

Chart II: Abstract of Descendants of John Eldred (1556-1632), Great Saxham-London, including emigrants to Pennsylvania.

(1) John Eldred   – Mary Revett   10 children.
     (1556-1632)   (? -1671)

(2) John Eldred   – Dorothy Goodwin   8 children.
     (1593-1649)

(3) Thomas Eldred   – Margaret Sanchey   3 children.
     (? -1691)

(4) John Eldred   – Mary Dodson   4 children.
     (? -1768)   (1727-82)

(5) Dodson Eldred   – Dinah Jarvis*   10 children.
     (1737-1816)   (1742-1821)

(6) Edward Jarvis Eldred – (1) Mary Payne (d. 1810 in England).
     (1763-1847)   4 children.
                            (2) Annie Northrup (m. in America).
                                  6 children.
     He emigrated to America in 1798 and purchased a large estate, 'Eldredville', in Lycoming County
     (later Sullivan County), Pennsylvania. Died at old house in Eckland, Lycoming County.

(7) William Eldred   – Annie Atkins   13 children.
     (1765-1842)   (d. 1836)

(8) William Eldred   – Sarah Meay (May)   7 children.
     (1788-1828)   (d. 1861 in
     Emigrated to   Philadelphia).
     Pennsylvania

*Dinah Jarvis was a granddaughter, through her mother, of William Penn, first governor of
Pennsylvania.

Chart III: *Selected Lines of Descent of John Eldred (1556-1632), London and Great Saxham, England-America (Pennsylvania).*

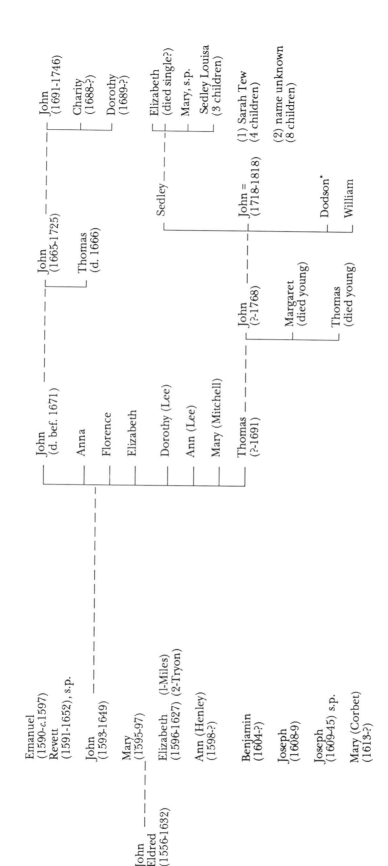

*See Chart IIIa.

Chart IIIa: Selected Lines of Descent of John Eldred (Continued)

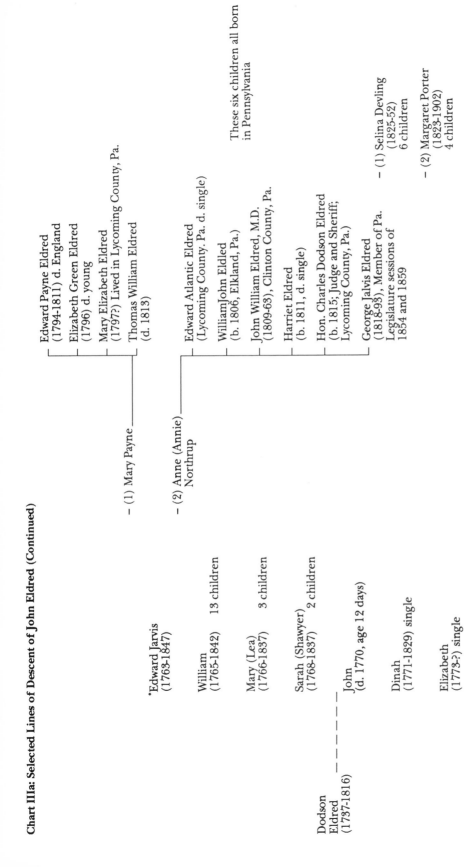

*Emigrant to America (Pennsylvania) in 1798.

Chart IV: Thomas Eldred (c.1537-c.1603), Ipswich, Suffolk, England

John Eldred (c.1415-89) — Corby, Lincolnshire and Knettishall, Suffolk
Reginald Eldred (?-1528) — Corby, Lincolnshire and Knettishall, Suffolk
Thomas Eldred (c.1460-1545) — Knettishall, Suffolk
Nicholas Eldred (1496-1566) — Knettishall, Suffolk

| William Eldred living in 1566 | Edmund Eldred, living in 1566; died 1569 in London of plague | Thomas Eldred, living in 1566 in Ipswich, Suffolk | Alice Eldred, m. Rookwood (Rookewood); living in 1566 |

Thomas Eldred of Ipswich, merchant, = Margery, daughter of Richard Studd (Stud) of Ipswich

Thomas Eldred of Ipswich, merchant, mariner (son of the Thomas Eldred above?); b. c.1537, d. before 1603. Sailed around world with Capt. Thomas Cavendish, 1586-88 (*Dictionary of National Biography*: Vol. XVIII, p.175). Issue: 12 children.

| Richard Eldred bapt. 8 Jan. 1559 St Mary-at-Quay's, Ipswich | Thomas Eldred of Ipswich = Susan, buried b. 24 Oct. 1561 bapt. at St Clements, 8 Nov. 1561, St;Mary- Ipswich, 27 at-Quay's, Ipswich; Oct. 1638 d. 1 May 1624, buried St Clement's, Ipswich, 3 May 1624; will proved 23 June 1624 | Christine Eldred, bapt. 11 May 1564, St Mary-at Quay's, Ipswich |

John Eldred, Esq. = Elizabeth, dau. of Colchester; b. of John Rusham, 21 Dec. 1565, in London; m. at Ipswich, moved to St Leonard, Colchester, Essex Colchester, in (1634); merchant, 1592; d. before alderman, J.P. her husband Bought manor of Olivers, Stanway, Essex. Arms granted 1630, established the Eldreds of Essex. Will, 11 Mar. 1643, d. 9 Oct. 1646. Will proved 21 Oct. 1646. Buried Colne, Essex

Mary = Henry Eldred Hamant b. 18 Nov. 1566

Margery = Edmund Eldred, Aldam bapt. 8 July 1568

Jane Eldred = Richard bapt. 22 Burlingame Sept. 1569

Susan Eldred = Samuel bapt. 3 Jan. Greene 1571

Philip Eldred = Anne gent. alderman. Survived twice mayor of her Hadleigh, Suffolk husband (1623 & 1627). Bapt. 8 Aug. 1572, St Mary-at-Quay's; d. 29 Feb. 1630, buried at Hadleisgh. Will proved 3 Mar. 1630. Established 'Eldreds of Hadleigh'

↑

William Eldred = (?)   Anne Eldred = Wade   Edward Eldred
bapt. 2 Dec. 1574,   bapt. 18 Sept.   bapt. 28 March
St Mary-at-Quay's;   1575   1577, St Mary-at-
d. before 23 June   Quay's
1624

Thomas Eldred of Ipswich and = Anna, dau. of Samuel
Barningham, b. c.1595; m.   Watson. Buried 27 Dec.
4 Feb, 1617; d. 1640, Ipswich   1642, Ipswich

| Thomas Eldred b. 20 Dec. 1617 | Charles Eldred of Ipswich, b. 3 Oct. 1619 = Susan Bridges, Colchester; m. Charles Eldred 24 June 1629, St Stephen's, Ipswich | Samuel Eldred of Ipswich, b. 27 Nov. 1620. Emigrated to America (Mass., and R.I.) 1640-1; d. c.1697, Kingstowne, R.I. Issue: 7 children = Elizabeth dau. of Daniel Miller, Needham Market, m. Samuel Eldred 25 Nov. 1640, St Mary-at-Quay's Ipswich | John Eldred | Mary Eldred bapt. 23 July 1626 |

Elizabeth Eldred
bapt. 1 May 1642,
St Nicholas, Ipswich

| Elizabeth Eldred, b. 26 Oct. 1642, Cambridge Mass. Prob. died young | Samuel Eldred, b. 2 Oct. 1644, Cambridge, Mass. d. 1720, Kingstowne, R.I. Issue: 3 children = Martha Knowles, dau. of Henry & Elizabeth (Potter) Knowles of R.I. b. 1651 d. 1728 | Mary Eldred b. 15 June 1646, Cambridge Mass. d. 1726, N. Kingstowne R.I. Issue: 6 children = prob. Rouse Helme, d. 17 May 1712, Kingstowne, R.I. | Thomas Eldred b. 8 Sept. 1648 Cambridge, Mass. d. 1726. N. Kingstowne R.I. Issue: 10 children = Susanna Cole (c.1653-1726), dau. of John and Susanna Hutchinson Cole, granddaughter of Anne Hutchinson (1591-1643), a martyr of religious liberty |

| James Eldred b. c.1650 Cambridge, Mass. No record of marriage. d. c.1687 | John Eldred b. 17 Aug. 1659, Chelsea Mass. d. Sept. 1724. N. Kingstowne, R.I. Issue: 9 children = Margaret Holden b. Jan. 1663, dau. of Randall & Frances (Dungan) Holden Frances was dau. of Lewis Latham, Falconer to Charles I. Margaret d. 1740 | Daniel Eldred (Eldredge) b. c.1663, Wickford, R.I., d. 18 Aug. 1726, N. Kingstowne, R.I. Issue: 10 children = Mary (Phillips?) b. c.1687. Her will was probated 24 Dec. 1750 |

*died after 1545

Chart V: John Eldred (1565-1646), Olivers, Stanway, Colchester; Essex, England

John Eldred (c.1415-89)	Corby, Lincolnshire and Knettishall, Suffolk
Reginald Eldred (?-1528)	Corby, Lincolnshire and Knettishall, Suffolk
Thomas Eldred (c.1460-aft.1545)	Knettishall, Suffolk
Nicholas Eldred (1496-1566)	Knettishall, Suffolk
Thomas Eldred (c.1537-c.1603)	Ipswich, Suffolk

John Eldred of Colchester, b. 1565, Merchant, Alderman, = Elizabeth, dau. of
J.P. (1634). Bought Manor of Olivers, John Rusham of London.
Stanway, Essex. Later lived in Little Birch Hall. Died before her
d. 9 Oct. 1646. Initially buried at Little Birch, husband
reinterred by grandson in church of Earl's Colne.
Arms-crest granted 14 Feb. 1630. Will dated 11 March
1643 and 24 Feb. 1645, pr. 21 Oct. 1646. Issue: 4
children, perhaps 7.

John Eldred of Colchester (1634), aft. of Olivers, Stanway, Essex. J.P., M.P., Collector of Sequestrations for Essex (1645) d. 16 Nov. 1682, buried at Colne 29 Nov. 1682. Issue: 8 children.	= Anne, dau. of Thomas Godman (Goodman) of Leatherhead, Surrey, d. 31 March 1678, d. age 72, buried at Earl's Colne	Edward Eldred	Mary Eldred Issue: 7 children: John Benjamin Joseph Eldred Samuel Thomas Elizabeth	= John Brand, Little Birch, Essex	Aquill Eldred d. 24 May 1681, aged 71 yrs. Buried at St Peter's Colchester = Edmund Thurston Gent. of Colchester

John Eldred of Olivers, b. 2 Oct. 1629, Colchester; Counselor at law, M.P. for Harwich in 1688 (defeated Pepys); d. 28 Sept. 1717. Buried Earl's Colne. Issue: 5 children: Elizabeth, John Margaret, John (of Olivers), Mary	= Margaret, dau. Richard and Mary (Denny) Harlackenden of Earl's Colne, Essex. Bapt. 11 June 1635; m. 15 Dec. 1657, Stanway Essex	Godman Eldred d. 1 Aug. 1649. Buried in St Swithen's London, Vis. Essex 1634	Edward Eldred d. Feb. 1683 Buried in St Dunstan's in the East. Vis. Essex 1668 Harleian Library, British Museum	Olive (Olivah) Eldred, d. Jan. 1697, St Albans Vis. Essex 1634	= Thomas Arris M.D. Dr. in Physick, fellow of College in London, J.P., Hertfordshire and Member of House of Commons

William Eldred, b. 1638, d. 3 May 1701, age 63 yrs. Buried Stanway, Essex. Monument in Stanway church. Vis. Essex 1668, Harleian Library, British Museum	= Joanna, dau. of John Goodwin, d. 15 July 1696 age 58 yrs. Buried at Stanway	Elizabeth Eldred, d. 10 June 1713. Vis. Essex 1668, Harleian Library, British Museum = Creithfield	Anne Eldred Vis. Essex 1664,1668 Harleian Library, British Museum	Marg Eldred d. 11 March 1701 at Lambourne, Essex; buried there. Vis. Essex 1668, Harleian Library, British Museum = Colman

John Eldred (1629-1717)

Elizabeth Eldred, b. 20 Apr. 1661, un-married, d. 24 April 1704, buried in St Margaret's Westminster	John Eldred, b. 26 March 1663, d. 21 Dec. 1664. Buried at Earl's Colne	Margaret Eldred, b. 27 June 1664; m. 29 Sept. 1707 at Earl's Colne	= Soloman Grimstone of Great Tey, Essex, Attorney at Law	John Eldred of Olivers, b. 1 Nov. 1666, m. 11 Feb. 1762 at Lincoln's Inn chapel; buried at Earl's Colne 14 Nov. 1732. Issue: 6 children	= Mary, dau. of Robert Horsman of Stratton, Rutland, half-sister of Richard Harlackenden of Earl's Colne, last male heir. She d. 29 May 1738, buried at Earl's Colne	Mary Eldred b. at Colne, bapt. 29 Nov. 1669 m. 29 Sept. 1707	= John Barfoot of Lincoln's Inn and Lambourne Hall

Horsman Eldred, b. 13 Dec. 1703, d. 2 Feb. 1704	Dulcebella Eldred, b. 10 Jan. Jan. 1704, d. unmarried 9 Feb., 1736 buried at Colne	John Eldred of Olivers, b. 7 Jan. 1705, d. 10 Oct. 1738. Buried at Colne, s.p. Last of the Eldreds of Olivers	= Susannah, dau. of Samuel Rawston of Lexden, Essex, d. 3 Apr. 17-? age 84 ,yrs. Buried at Earl's Colne	Anne Eldred, b. 20 Dec. 1706, m. 4 Jan. 1738, d. 10 Feb. 1770, buried at Earl's Colne	= John Wale of Earl's Colne; d. 22 March 1761, buried there	Mary Eldred b. 9 June 1708, d. 27 Feb. 1736, buried at Earl's Colne	Edward Eldred b. 24 Sept. 1715 d. 27 Sept. 1715

* It is possible that Thomas Eldred's father was Nicholas Eldred, but positive proof is lacking. He is the founder of the Eldred family in Essex.

Index

(Compiled by Auriol Griffith Jones)

Note: For obvious reasons of space not all Eldreds are indexed. In general, an individual is included when there is significant information about him; and/or the name of the spouse is given, in order that other families may trace their connections.

The appendixes, pedigrees and illustrations are not indexed.

South East Essex College
of Arts & Technology
Luker Road Southend-on-Sea Essex SS1 1ND
Tel: (01702) 220400 Fax: (01702) 432320 Minicom: (01702) 22064